I0803880

CHRIST AND THE SPIRITUAL WORLD
THE QUEST FOR THE HOLY GRAIL

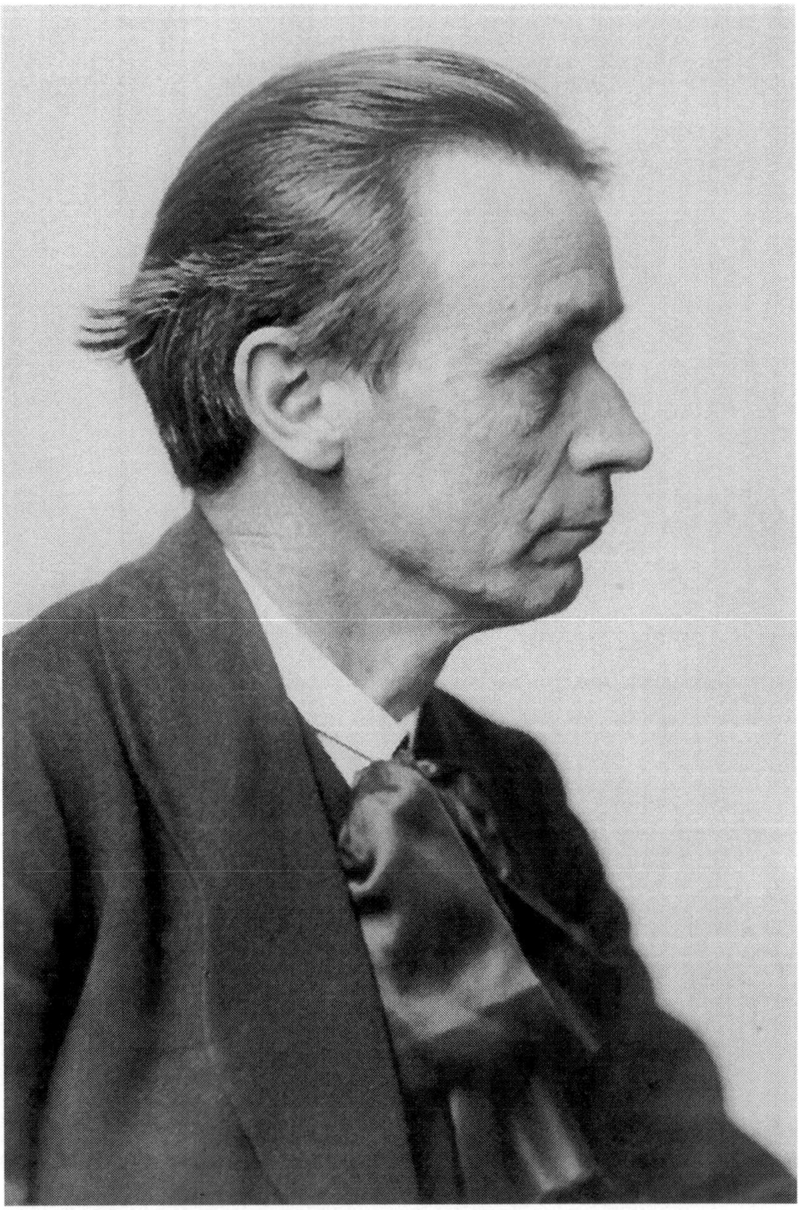

CHRIST AND THE SPIRITUAL WORLD
THE QUEST FOR THE HOLY GRAIL

A course of six lectures held in Leipzig between
28 December 1913 and 2 January 1914

TRANSLATED BY CHARLES DAVY AND FREDERICK AMRINE

EDITED AND INTRODUCED BY FREDERICK AMRINE

RUDOLF STEINER

RUDOLF STEINER PRESS

CW 149

Rudolf Steiner Press
Hillside House, The Square
Forest Row, RH18 5ES
www.rudolfsteinerpress.com

Published by Rudolf Steiner Press 2022

Originally published in German under the title *Christus und die geistigen Welt. Von der Suche nach dem heiligen Gral* (volume 149 in the *Rudolf Steiner Gesamtausgabe* or Collected Works) by Rudolf Steiner Verlag, Dornach. Based on shorthand notes that were not reviewed or revised by the speaker. This authorized translation is based on the sixth German edition (1987), edited by Robert Friedenthal

Published by permission of the Rudolf Steiner Nachlassverwaltung, Dornach

A catalogue record for this book is available from the British Library

ISBN 978 1 85584 605 0

Cover by Morgan Creative
Typeset by Symbiosys Technologies, Vishakapatnam, India
Printed and bound by 4Edge Ltd., Essex

CONTENTS

PUBLISHER'S NOTE

THIS lecture course took place at a time when Rudolf Steiner had separated himself and the German Section from the Theosophical Society (based in Adyar, India). The Anthroposophical Society had been founded, with its first assembly having taken place on 3 February 1913. The announcement of November 1913 in the *Mitteilungen für die Mitglieder der Anthroposophischen Gesellschaft* ('Notifications for the members of the Anthroposophical Society') no. IV, published by Mathilde Scholl, read: 'From 28 December 1913 to 4 January 1914 Dr Rudolf Steiner will hold a cycle of lectures and two public lectures in Leipzig…'. The titles of the public lectures were 'Spiritual Science and the Spiritual World. Perspectives on the Goals of Our Time' (3 January 1914), and 'Theosophy as a Benefit for Life' (4 January 1914). The lectures which make up *Christ and the Spiritual World* were the final lectures by Rudolf Steiner that were heard by the poet Christian Morgenstern, shortly before his death. They inspired him to write the poem 'Er sprach… Und wie er sprach, erschien in ihm der Tierkreis, Cherubim und Seraphim…' in *Wir fanden einen Pfad* ('He spoke… And as he spoke, the zodiac appeared in him, Cherubim and Seraphim...', from 'We Have Found a Path'). It was also on the occasion of these lectures that a meeting took place between Christian Morgenstern and the Russian novelist Andrei Bely.

Introduction

Rudolf Steiner begins this cycle of lectures with a disconcerting promise not to provide answers, but rather to make us 'disturbingly aware of how contradictions, difficulties, must pile up before the soul of anyone who wants to accept in the right sense our anthroposophical knowledge concerning humanity in the evolution of the world'. It seems that to be an anthroposophist implies not the comfortable possession of some set of truths, but rather incessant wrestling with difficulties and outright contradictions.

He embarks on an account of the Christ-Impulse—itself an utterly enigmatic designation—that makes no mention of the Church, or indeed of any Christian denomination. He refers to only one theologian by name, Paul, but not to any of his actual theology. Ironically, he asserts that all of theology is better suited to block understanding of the Christ-Impulse than to promote it. Of the Bible itself, Steiner asks about what is missing: for example, what became of the Three Magi?

He provides a lengthy and sympathetic account of Gnosticism. But the Gnostics are problematical in two senses: not only do their elaborate thought constructs appear childishly fanciful to modern-day Darwinian monists, but—unspoken in the lecture—their thinking also proves anathema to Christian theologians. The Gnostics are the arch-heretics. So what Steiner depicts as the subtlest manifestation of the deepening of thought that occurred in the fourth post-Atlantean epoch is directly opposed to the theological understanding—or I should say, the theological misunderstanding—of the Mystery of Golgotha. But it is not enough simply to understand and accept the Gnostics' account, for even their thinking is grossly inadequate to the task. Steiner ends the first lecture by expressing the disheartening conclusion that even Gnosticism is not the solution to the problem; it is, rather, the keenest exemplar of the problem itself.

The Mystery of Golgotha, Steiner's term for what is usually described as the Passion, is precisely a Mystery in the strictest sense. Even though it is performed publicly, only a tiny circle of people actually witnesses it. And its meaning remains totally inaccessible to human conceptual thinking.

'The Christ-Impulse' is shown to be not a poorly chosen metaphor, but a precise description. Like an impulse in physics, the Christ-Impulse is a *force* that makes things happen in the world. The Christ-Impulse is, among many other things, the ultimate cause of the extraordinary blossoming of free, human thinking that takes place in the fourth post-Atlantean epoch.

Earlier epochs, especially that led by the holy rishis, would surely have understood the import of the Christ-Impulse. But Christ did not incarnate then. He incarnated only when human thinking had become autonomous, had become free. But again, paradoxically, thinking purchased its freedom by being cut off from reality. In our thinking, we live isolated on an island. The Christ-Impulse came to *enact* human freedom, even if that meant that humanity would be cut off from any conceptual understanding of the Christ-Impulse.

Moreover, the Christ-Impulse is shown to be not a one-time event, beginning with the Incarnation, but rather a continuous process that was at work eons earlier. In his third lecture, Steiner outlines three 'pre-earthly deeds of Christ' that healed potential imbalances in human nature. The image of St George defeating the dragon bears reminiscences of these events.

Who comes closest in this cycle of lectures to grasping the reality of the Mystery of Golgotha? Three figures stand out as the main protagonists. Two of the three, Parsifal and Joan of Arc, have effectively no philosophical or theological understanding of the Christ-Impulse. But they help to enact it. The third, Kepler, arrives at certain theological insights not by pursuing theology as such, but rather through the back door of mathematics and astronomy.

The final two lectures provide a rare account of the process Steiner underwent in performing esoteric research into the saga of Parsifal. However difficult it may be to emulate, surely Steiner gives this account as a model that may encourage us to perform our own original, esoteric research. Anthroposophy is, after all, about *knowing* rather than *believing*.

Frederick Amrine
June 2022

Lecture 1

LEIPZIG, 28 DECEMBER 1913

MANY people who are naturally fitted to receive anthroposophy in our present age will find it necessary to clear away various contradictions that may arise in their minds. In particular, the soul can be brought up against a certain contradiction when it wants to take seriously the memories of such a festive season as that which includes Christmas and the New Year. When we take these memories seriously, then it becomes clear to us that at the same time as we try to gain knowledge, we must penetrate into the spiritual history of humanity if we are to understand rightly our own spiritual evolution. We need only take a certain thought, and we shall find it on the one hand full of light, while on the other it makes us disturbingly aware of how contradictions, difficulties, must pile up before the soul of anyone who wants to accept in the right sense our anthroposophical knowledge concerning humanity and the evolution of the world.

Among the varied forms of knowledge that we try to reach through our anthroposophical studies we must of course include knowledge of the Christ; knowledge of the fundamentally important impulse—we have called it the Christ-Impulse[1]—which came in at the beginning of our era. And we are bound often to ask ourselves how we can hope to penetrate more effectively, with deepened anthroposophical knowledge, into the course of human evolution, in order to understand the Christ-Impulse, than those who lived at the time of the Mystery of Golgotha[2] were able to do. Was it not much easier for them to penetrate into this Mystery,[3] whose secret is specially bound up with the evolution of humanity, than it is for us, at this great distance in time? That might be a troublesome question for persons of the present who want to seek an understanding of

Christ in the light of anthroposophy. It might become one of those contradictions that have a depressing effect just when we want to take most earnestly the deeper principles of our anthroposophical knowledge. This contradiction can be cleared away only when we call up before our souls the whole spiritual situation of humanity at the beginning of our era.

If we try—at first without any kind of religious or similar feeling—to enter into the psychic disposition of humanity at that time, we can make a most peculiar discovery. We can say to ourselves that we will rely on what cannot be denied even by minds most given over to externals; we will draw on the old tradition as found in history, but we will try to penetrate into that part of it which embraces the purest spiritual life. In this way we may hope to lay hold of essential elements in the evolution of humanity. Let us therefore try to enter quite historically into the endeavours that were made, say two hundred years before the Mystery of Golgotha and a hundred and fifty years after it, to deepen our thinking in order to understand the secrets, the riddles, of the world. Then we realize that during the centuries before and after the Mystery of Golgotha a change of far-reaching significance occurred in human souls with regard to the life of thought. We find that a large part of the realized world received the influence of that which Greek culture and other deepened forms of thinking had achieved some centuries previously.

When we consider what humanity had accomplished in this way by its own efforts, not in response to any impulse from without, and how much had been attained by those who were called 'sages' in the Stoic[4] sense (and a good many personalities in Roman history were so ranked), then we are bound to say: These conquests in the realm of thought and ideas were made at the beginning of our era, and Western life has not added very much to them. We have gained an endless amount of knowledge concerning the facts of nature and have been through revolutions in our ways of thinking about the external world. But the thoughts, the ideas themselves, through which these advances have been made, and with which we have tried to discern the secrets of existence in external, spatial terms, have really developed very little since the beginning of our era. They were all present—even those of which the modern world is so proud, including the idea of evolution—in the souls of that period. What might be called an intellectual laying hold of the world, a life of ideas, had reached a certain summit, and not only among particular individuals, such as the pupils of Socrates[5] a little earlier; it had become popular in a limited sense and had spread widely over Southern Europe and other regions. This deepening of thought is truly astonishing.

An impartial history of philosophy would have to pay special attention to this triumph of human thinking at that time.

But if we now take these highly significant advances in the realm of ideas, and on the other hand the secrets bound up with the Mystery of Golgotha, we become aware of something different. We realize that as the story of the event on Golgotha became known in that age, an immense wrestling of thought with that Mystery occurred. We see how the philosophies of the period, especially the Gnostic philosophy in its much profounder form, struggled to bring all the ideas it had gained to bear on this one purpose. And it is most important to let this struggle work upon us. For we then come to recognize that the struggle was in vain; that this immense deepening of thinking that humanity had achieved was indeed there, and indeed made every effort to comprehend the Mystery of Golgotha, but that none of these efforts were sufficient. The Mystery of Golgotha appeared to human understanding as though it were dispersed through far-distant spiritual worlds, and would not unveil itself.

Now from the outset I would like to say that when in these lectures I speak of the Mystery of Golgotha, I do not wish to invest this term with any colouring drawn from religious traditions or convictions. We shall be concerned purely with objective facts that are fundamental to human evolution, and with what physical and spiritual observation can bring to light. I shall leave aside everything that individual religious creeds have to say about the Mystery of Golgotha and shall look only at what has happened in the course of human evolution. I shall have to say many things which will be made clear and substantiated later on.

In setting the Mystery of Golgotha by the side of the deepest thought of that time, the first thing that strikes one is what I expressed by saying: The nature of this Mystery lies far, far beyond what can be reached by the development of thinking. And the more exactly one studies this contrast, the more is one brought to the following recognition. One can enter deeply into the thought-world that belongs to the beginning of our era; one can try to bring livingly before one's soul what thinking meant for those denizens of Greece and Rome; one can call up before one's soul the ideas that sprang from their thinking, and then one comes to the feeling: Yes, that was the time when thought underwent an unprecedented deepening. Something happened with thought; it approached the human soul in a quite new way. But when one wants to make fully alive inwardly what can be called the clairvoyant faculty, what one was able to call before the soul about this deepening of thought and vitalization of the world of thought of that time; when one bears that in one's soul, and allows it to become effective in the soul, then suddenly something surprising emerges. One feels that something is happening far, far away in the spiritual worlds and that the deepening of thought is a consequence of it.

We have already called attention to the fact that behind our world lie other worlds—the astral,[6] the devachanic, and the higher devachanic.[7] Let us first remind ourselves that these three worlds lie behind our own. Then, if the clairvoyant state of soul is raised to full activity within oneself, the impression is received that neither in the astral world nor in the lower devachanic world can a complete explanation of the deepening of thought at that time be found. Only if one could place one's soul in the higher devachanic world—so says clairvoyant insight—would one experience what it is that streams through the other two worlds and penetrates right down into our physical world. In our physical world it is recognizable as the radical transformation of the world of thought throughout the centuries.

One can initially only transport oneself to the physical world and its consideration. On this physical plane there is no need to be aware, while steeping oneself in that past world of ideas, of anything told concerning the Mystery of Golgotha. One can leave that quite out of account and ask simply: No matter what happened over there in Palestine, what does external history indicate? It shows that in Greece and Rome an infinite deepening of thought took place. Let us put a circle round this Greek and Roman thought-world and make it an enclosed island, as it were, in our life of soul—an island shut off from everything outside; let us imagine that no report of the Mystery of Golgotha has reached it. Then, when we inwardly contemplate this world, we certainly find there nothing that is known today about the Mystery of Golgotha, but we find an infinite deepening of thought which indicates that here in the evolution of humanity something happened which took hold of the innermost being of the soul on the physical plane. We are persuaded that in no previous age and among no other people had thinking ever been like that! However sceptical people may be, however little they may care to know about the Mystery of Golgotha, they must admit one thing—that in this island world that we have enclosed there was a deepening of thought never previously known.

But if one places oneself in this thought-world, and has a clairvoyant faculty in the background, then one feels truly immersed in the individual character of this thought. And then one says to oneself: Yes, as this thinking flowers into idea, with Plato[8] and others, as it passes over into the world we tried to enclose, it has a quality which sets the soul free, which lays hold of the soul and brings it to a loftier view of itself. Whatever else you may apprehend in the external world or in the spiritual world makes you dependent on those worlds; in thinking you take hold of something which lives in you and which you can experience completely. You may draw back from the physical world, you may disbelieve in a spiritual world, you may refuse to know anything about clairvoyant impressions, you may shut out all physical impressions—with thoughts you can live in yourself; in your thinking you lay hold, as it were, of your own being!

One can have this insight. But then—and it cannot be otherwise if one enters with clairvoyant perception into this sea of thought, as I might call it—a feeling of the isolation of thought comes over one; a feeling that thought is still only thought; that it lives first of all only in the soul, and that one cannot draw from it the power to go out into a world where the ground of the rest of our being—the ground of what else we are—is to be found. In the very moment when one discerns the grandeur of thought, one discerns also its unreality. Then one can see also how in the surrounding world that one has come to know through clairvoyance, there is fundamentally nothing to sustain thought.

Then why should thought be there at all? The physical world can do nothing but falsify it. Those who wish to be pure materialists, who refuse to ascribe to thought any primal reality of its own, should really prefer to prohibit it. For if the natural world is the only real world, thought can only falsify it. It is only because materialists are illogical that they do not embrace the only theory of cognition that goes with monistic[9] materialism—the refrain-from-thinking, think-no-more theory. But to those who immerse themselves with clairvoyant perception in the world of thought there comes this disquieting awareness of the isolation of thought, as though they were standing quite alone with it. And then only one thing remains for them; but it does remain. Something comes towards them, even though it be from a far spiritual distance, separated from them by two worlds; and it becomes apparent—so the clairvoyant soul says to itself—that in this third world lies the true origin, the fountain-head, of that which is in the life of thought. For clairvoyant souls in our time it could be a powerful experience to immerse themselves, alone with their thinking, in the time when thought underwent its deepening; to shut out everything else, including knowledge of the Mystery of Golgotha, and to reflect how the thought-content on which we still nourish ourselves came forth in the Graeco-Roman world.

Then one should turn one's gaze to other worlds and feel rising over the devachanic world a star that belongs to a higher spiritual world; the star from which rays out the power that makes itself felt in the thought-world of Graeco-Roman antiquity. Then one feels oneself here on Earth, but carried away from the world of today and plunged into the Graeco-Roman world, with its influence spreading out over other regions at that time, before the Mystery of Golgotha. But as soon as one lets the spiritual world make its impression on one, there appears again, shining over devachan, the star (I speak symbolically), or the spiritual being of whom one says to oneself: Yes, the experience of the isolation of thought, and of the possibility of thought having undergone such a deepening at the beginning of our era—this is a consequence of the rays that shine out from this star in the higher spiritual world.

And then comes a feeling which at first knows nothing of the historical tradition of the Mystery of Golgotha but can be expressed thus: Yes, you are there in the Graeco-Roman world of ideas, with all that Plato and others were able to give to the general education of humanity, with what they have imparted to human souls—you feel yourself living in the midst of that. And then you wait ... and truly not in vain, for as though deep in the background of spiritual life appears the star which sends forth its rays of power; and you can say that what you have experienced is a result of these rays of power.

This experience can be gone through. And in going through it one has not relied on any kind of tradition, but has quite impartially sought the origin of what took place in the Graeco-Roman world. But one has also had the experience of being separated by three worlds from understanding the root-causes of that Graeco-Roman world.

And then, perhaps, one turns to the people of that time who tried in their own way to understand the change. Even the external scholarship of today has come to recognize that in this period of transition at the beginning of our era some religious-philosophic geniuses lived. And they can best be encountered by looking at Gnosticism. The Gnosis is known in the most varied ways. Externally, remarkably little is really known about it, but from the available documents one can still get an impression of its endless depth. We will speak of it only in so far as it bears on our present considerations.

Above all we can say that the Gnostics had a feeling for what I have just described: that for the causes of what happened in that past epoch one must look to worlds lying infinitely far away in the background. This awareness was passed on to others, and if we are not superficial we can, if we will, see it glimmering through what we may call the theology of Paul, and in many other manifestations also.

Now, anyone who steeps themselves in the Gnosis of that period will have great difficulty in understanding it. Our souls are too much affected and infected by the fruits of the materialistic developments of the last few centuries. In tracing back the evolution of the world they are too readily inclined to think in terms of the Kant-Laplace theory of a cosmic nebula,[10] of something purely material. And even those who seek for a more spiritual conception of the world—even they, when they look back to the beginning of time, think of this cosmic nebula or something similar. These modern people, even the most spiritual, feel very happy when they are spared the trouble of discerning the spiritual in the primal beginnings of cosmic evolution. They find it a great relief, these souls of today, when they can say to themselves: 'This or that rarefied form of material substance was there to start with, and out of it everything spiritual developed side by side with everything physical.' And so we often find souls who are greatly comforted when they can apply the most materialistic methods of inquiry to the beginning of the cosmos and arrive at the most abstract conception of some kind of gaseous body.

That is why it is so difficult to enter into the thoughts of the Gnosis. For what the Gnosis places at the beginning of the world carries no suggestion of anything at all material. People thoroughly attuned to modern education will perhaps be unable to restrain a slight smile if they are invited to think in the sense of the Gnosis that the world in which they find themselves, the world they explain so beautifully with his Darwinism,[11] bears no relation to a true picture of how the world began. Indeed, they will hardly be able to help smiling when they are asked to think that the origin of the world resides in that cosmic being who is beyond all concepts, not to be reached by any of the means that are applied nowadays to explaining the world. In the primal Divine Father—says the Gnosis—lies the ground of the world, and only in what proceeds from Him do we find something to which the soul can struggle through if it turns away from all material conceptions and searches a little for its own innermost depth. And this is silence: the eternal silence in which there is neither space nor time, but silence only.

It was to this duality of the primal Father and the silence preceding time and space that the Gnostics looked up; and then, from the union of the primal Father with the silence, as it were, they conceived other existences proceeding: one can equally well call them worlds or beings. And from them others, and again others, and again others—and so on through thirty stages. And only at the thirtieth stage did the Gnostic posit a condition prior to our present mentality—a condition so delightfully explained by Darwinism in terms of that mentality. Or, strictly speaking, at the thirty-first stage, for thirty of these existences, which can be called worlds or beings, precede our world. 'Aeon' is the name generally given to these thirty beings or worlds that precede our own.

One can get a clear idea of what is meant by this Aeon-world only by saying to oneself: To the thirty-first stage there belongs not only what your senses perceive as the external world, but also the way in which your thinking as a physical human being tries to explain the sense world. It is easy enough to come to terms with a spiritual conception of the world if one says: Yes, the external world is certainly *maya*,[12] but with thinking we penetrate into a spiritual world—and if one hopes that this thinking really can reach the spiritual world. But according to the Gnostic this is not so; for him, this thinking belongs to the thirty-first Aeon, to the physical world. So not only sense perception, but human thinking, lies outside the thirty Aeons, who can be looked up to through the stages of spiritual evolution, and who reveal themselves in ever-mounting perfection.

One can easily imagine the smile that comes to a monist, standing at the summit of his time, if he is asked to believe in thirty preceding worlds—thirty worlds with a content entirely different from anything his thinking can conceive. But that was the view of the Gnostics. And then they asked themselves: How is it with *this* world?

We will disregard for a while what we have ourselves said about the world in the sense of the early twentieth century. What I am now telling you must not be taken as offering a convincing world-picture. In the anthroposophy of the twentieth century we have naturally to get beyond the Gnosis, but just now we want to sink ourselves into it.

Why is this surrounding world, including the human faculty of thinking about it, shut off from the thirty Aeons? We must look, said the Gnostic, to the lowest but still purely spiritual Aeon. And there we find the Divine Sophia, the Divine Wisdom. She had evolved in a spiritual way through the twenty-nine stages, and in the spiritual world she looked up to the highest Aeon through the ranks of spiritual beings or worlds. But one day, one cosmic day, it became evident to her that if she was to maintain a free vision into the spiritual world of the Aeons, she had to separate something from herself. And she separated from herself that which existed in her as desire. And this desire, being no longer present in the Divine Sophia, the Divine Wisdom, now wanders through the realms of space and permeates everything that comes into being in the realms of space. Desire does not live only in sense perception, but also in human thinking, and in the longing that looks back to the spiritual world; but always as something cast out into human souls. As her image, but as an image of the Divine Sophia cast out from her, lives this desire, Achamod, thrown out into the world and permeating it.

If you look into yourself, without raising yourself into spiritual worlds, you look into the desire-filled world of Achamod. Because this world is filled with desire, it cannot disclose within itself what is revealed by looking out into the world of the Aeons. Far, far away in the world of the Aeons—so thought the Gnosis—the pure spirituality of the Aeons engenders what the Gnostics called the Son of the Father-God, and also what they called the pure Holy Spirit. So we have here another generation, as it were, another evolutionary line, different from that which led to the Divine Sophia. As in the propagation of physical life, the sexes are separate, so in the progression of the Aeons another stream took its origin from a very high level in the spiritual world: the stream of the Son and the Holy Spirit stemming from the Father. So in the world of Aeons there was one stream leading to the Divine Sophia and another to the Son and the Holy Spirit. If one rises through the Aeons, one comes eventually to an Aeon from whom there arose on the one hand the succession leading to the Divine Sophia, and on the other the succession leading to the Son and the Holy Spirit. And then we ascend to the Father-God and the Divine Silence.

Because the human soul is translated with Achamod into the material world, it has in the sense of the Gnosis a longing for the spiritual world, and above all for the Divine Sophia, from whom it is separated through being filled with Achamod. This feeling of being separated from the Divine, of not being within the Divine—this feeling is actually experienced, according to the Gnostics, as the material world. And the Gnostic sees originating from the divine-spiritual world, but bound up with Achamod, what one might call (to borrow a Greek word) the Demiurge,[13] the cosmic Architect.

This Demiurge is the real arch-creator and sustainer of what is permeated with Achamod and the material. Human souls are woven into his world. But they are imbued also with longing for the Divine Sophia. As though in the far distance of the Aeon-world appear the Son and the Holy Spirit in their pure divine spirituality, but they appear only to persons who have—in the sense of the Gnosis—raised themselves above everything in which is embodied Achamod, the desire that pervades space.

Why is there this longing in the souls that have been drawn into the world of Achamod? Why, after their separation from the divine-spiritual world, do they feel a longing for it? The Gnostics also asked themselves these questions, and they said: Achamod was cast out from the Divine Wisdom, the Divine Sophia, but before Achamod had completely become this material world, where we now live, there came to her something like a brief raying-out of light from the Son of God; and then immediately the light vanished again. For the Gnostic this was an important concept: that Achamod—the same Achamod that lives in the souls of human beings—had been granted in the primal remote past a glimpse of divine light, which had then immediately disappeared. But the memory of it lives on today in human souls, however deeply enmeshed in the material world the soul may be. 'I live in the world of Achamod, the material world', such a soul might have said. 'I am surrounded with a sheath drawn from the material world, but when I sink into my inner being, a memory comes to life within me. The element that holds me bound to the material world longs after the Divine Sophia, the Divine Wisdom; for the being of Achamod, which lives in me, was once illuminated by a ray from the Son of God, who dwells in the world of the Aeons.'

We should try to picture clearly to ourselves such a soul as this, a disciple of the Gnosis. There were such souls; they are not a hypothetical invention. Anyone who studies history with understanding will come to realize through the external documents that many souls of this kind lived in that period.

We need to see clearly why there are such strong objections nowadays to what I have been saying. What will a thoroughly level-headed person of today have to say about the Gnosis? We have already had to listen to the view that the theology of Paul gives an impression of rabbinical subtleties, far too intricate for a sensible monist to concern himself with—a monist who looks out proudly over the world and draws it all together with the simple concept of evolution or with the still simpler concept of energy, and says: 'Now at last we have grown up; we have acquired the ideas which give us a picture of the world based on energy, and we look back at these children, these poor dear children, who centuries ago built up the Gnosis out of childishness—they imagined all sorts of spirits, thirty Aeons! That is what the human soul does in its time of nursery play. The grown-up soul of today, with its far-reaching monism, has left such fancies far behind. We must look back indulgently at these Gnostic infantilisms—they are really charming!'

Such is the prevailing mood today, and it is not easily teachable. One might say to it: Yes, if a Gnostic, with his soul born out of the Gnosis, were to stand before you, he might also take the liberty of expressing his outlook, somewhat like this: 'I understand very well how you have become so proud and arrogant, with your ideas of evolution and energy, but this is because your thinking has become so crude and simple and primitive that you are satisfied with your nebulae and your entirely abstract concepts. You say the words "evolution" and "energy" and think you have got something, but you are blind to the finer spiritual life that seeks its way up into that which rises through thirty stages above anything you have.'

But for us the antithesis mentioned at the beginning of this lecture becomes all the sharper. We see on the one hand our own time, with its quite crude and primitive concepts, and on the other the Gnosis. And we have seen how the Gnosis employs endlessly complicated concepts—thirty Aeons—in order to find in the course of evolution the Son of God and the Holy Spirit, and to find in the soul the longing for the Divine Sophia and the Holy Spirit.

Then we ask ourselves: Is it not from the deepening of thought in the Graeco-Roman world that we have gained what we have carried so splendidly far in our thoughts about energy and evolution? And in this Gnosis, with its complicated ideas, so unsympathetic to the present day, are we not looking at something quite strange? Are not these colossal contrasts? Indeed they are. And the contradiction, lying like a weight on the soul, becomes even greater if we reflect on what was said about clairvoyant souls: that they can transpose themselves into the thought-world of the Greeks and Romans, and then see the world with the star, of which we have spoken. And mingled everywhere with this deepening of Greek thought we find that other deepening which the Gnosis exemplifies. Yet when we look at this with the aid of what anthroposophy should give us today, and are yet powerless to understand what the star should signify, separated as we are from it by three worlds—and if we ask the Gnostics: Have you understood what happened at that time in the historical evolution of humanity? ... then, standing on the ground of anthroposophy, we cannot take the answer from the Gnostics, for it could never satisfy us; it would throw no light on what is shown to the clairvoyant soul.

It is not my wish that you should treat our considerations today as offering an explanation of anything. The more you feel that what I have told you is not an explanation; the more you feel that I have put before you contradiction after contradiction and have shown you only *one* occult experience, the perception of the star, the better will you have understood me for today. I would wish you to see clearly that at the beginning of our era there appeared in the world something which influenced human understanding and was yet far, far from being understood; I would like you to feel that the period at the beginning of our era was a great riddle. I want you to feel that in human evolution there happened something which seemed at first like a deepening of thought, or a discovery of thought; and that the root-causes of this are a profound enigma. You must seek in hidden worlds for that which appeared in the *maya* of the physical sense-world as a deepening of Graeco-Roman thought. And it is not an explanation of what we have heard, but the setting out of a riddle, that I wished to give you today. We will continue tomorrow.

Lecture 2

LEIPZIG, 29 DECEMBER 1913

If we call to mind once more the thoughts of yesterday's lecture, we can draw them together by saying that the period at the beginning of our era took all possible pains to understand the Mystery of Golgotha out of the treasure of its wisdom, and that this endeavour encountered the very greatest difficulties. We must pause to consider this, for unless we are clear about this inevitable misunderstanding of what came about through the Mystery of Golgotha, we shall not be able to comprehend an essential fact of later centuries: the advent of the idea of the Grail, concerning which we shall have something to say in connection with our subject.

When we recall the beginning of our era and look at its most significant, wisdom-filled current of thought—when we look, that is, at the Gnostics—then on the one hand we can see, in the light of yesterday's lecture, how grandly original were the ideas with which they sought to place the Son of God in the centre of an imposing world-picture. But if on the other hand we look at what can be learnt about the Mystery of Golgotha from the spiritual chronicle of the time, then we must say that no real truth can be had from the concepts and ideas of the Gnostics. And this is particularly evident when we consider the various ways in which the Gnostics pictured the manifestation of the Christ in Jesus of Nazareth.

There were some Gnostics who said: 'Yes, Christ is a Being who transcends everything earthly and comes from spiritual realms; such a Being can remain for only a limited time in a human body, as was the body of Jesus of Nazareth.' These Gnostics had discerned something which today we must emphasize again and again: that in truth the Christ Being dwelt for three years only in the body of Jesus of

Nazareth. But these Gnostics went wrong over the way in which the Christ Being dwelt in the body of Jesus. First of all, the mystery of the body of Jesus of Nazareth was not clear to them. They did not know that the ego of Zarathustra had lived in this body; that the three bodies of Jesus of Nazareth represented in their conjunction an essence of humanity which had never before been incarnated in the flesh on Earth. The whole relation of the Christ to the two Jesus-boys[14] was hidden from these Gnostics. Hence they were never satisfied—or at least their followers were never satisfied—with what they could say about the temporary inhabiting of the body of Jesus of Nazareth by Christ.

Another question touched on by the Gnostics was the manner of the birth of Christ, the most tremendous Mystery in human evolution. They knew well enough that the necessary reason for the appearance of Christ on Earth is connected with the passage through conception in the flesh, but they could not quite see how to bring the mother of Jesus into relation with the birth of Christ. And those who tried to work this out—there were some—were very little understood.

Again, there were Gnostics who because of these various difficulties denied entirely that the Christ had appeared on Earth in bodily form. They formed the idea that it was only a phantom body—what we should call an astral body—which had gone about on Earth before and after the death on Golgotha; it had appeared here and there, but it was not a physical body. Because of the difficulty of conceiving how the Christ could have been united with a physical body, it was said that no such union had occurred and that when people thought He had gone about in a physical body, this was illusion, *maya*. This notion, too, gained no recognition. So we can see everywhere that the Gnostics tried to master with their concepts the greatest historical Mystery in the Earth's evolution, but their ideas were inadequate, powerless in face of what had actually occurred.

Now we must speak of the way in which Paul tried to come to terms with the problem, but first it will be well to grasp clearly how it was that such misunderstandings were inevitable. If with the help of spiritual investigation we ask ourselves a series of questions and try to answer them, the course of events will become apparent to us in—one might say—an abstract form.

For example, we can ask: If the epoch of Jesus Christ was so poorly equipped to understand His nature, would another epoch have been in a position to understand Him? If as a spiritual investigator one enters into human souls at different periods of the past, one certainly comes to a strange result. First of all, one can enter into the souls of the great teachers of the Ancient Indian civilization, the first of the post-Atlantean cultural epochs. There, as we have often emphasized, we stand with deepest admiration before the comprehensive, deeply-grounded wisdom, permeated throughout with clairvoyant vision, of the Indian holy rishis[15] of that ancient time. We know that the souls of those great teachers were open to cosmic mysteries which were lost to the wisdom of later times. And when one tries to enter clairvoyantly, as well as one can, into the soul of one of these great teachers of Ancient India, one must say that if it had been possible for the Christ Being to have appeared on Earth among the holy rishis at that time, their wisdom would have been in the highest degree capable of understanding the nature of Christ. Then there would have been no difficulties; they would have known what it was all about. And since one cannot properly express in abstract words such significant phenomena as those I have just described, let me evoke a picture.

If the holy rishis of Ancient India had perceived in someone the splendour of the wisdom of the Logos, the wisdom that pulses through the world, they would have brought to the Logos their offering of frankincense, symbolising a recognition of the divine that works in the realms of humanity. But the Christ Being could find no body at that period; the bodies of that time would not have been suitable for Him. So He could not appear—the reasons for this will be given later—in the epoch when all the means of understanding were present.

If we go further and enter into the souls of the old Zarathustrian civilization, we can say: These souls were certainly not endowed with the high spiritual resources of the Ancient Indian civilization, but they would have understood that the Spirit of the Sun had elected to live in a human body, and they would have been able to grasp the significance of this fact in relation to the Sun-Spirit. To speak pictorially again: the disciples of Zarathustra would have honoured their Sun-Spirit with an offering of shining gold, the symbol of wisdom.

If we go further still into the Chaldean-Egyptian cultural epoch,[16] we find that the possibility of understanding Christ Jesus would have again decreased; but it would not have narrowed down as far as it did in the fourth post-Atlantean epoch, the Graeco-Latin epoch,[17] when even Gnosticism was not powerful enough to understand this manifestation. It would have been understood that a star from spiritual heights had appeared and had been born in a human being. This divine, spiritual line of descent from spheres beyond the earthly would have been clearly grasped; and myrrh would have been brought as an offering. And if we enter into the souls of those who figure in the Bible as the three Magi, who come from the East and are the guardians of the treasures of wisdom derived from the three preceding cultural-epochs, we find the Bible itself indicating that a certain understanding was present, since these three Magi do at least appear at the birth of the Jesus-child.

One thing that very few people think about today will certainly strike us—that the Bible is in a strange position with regard to the three Magi. For does it not wish to say that here were three men of exceptional wisdom who even at the time of the birth understood its significance? But one might ask—where were the Three Wise Men later on? What came of their wisdom in the end? Have we anything that could lead us back to an understanding of Christ's manifestation by way of these Three Wise Men? This has to be thrown out only as a question. It is one of the many questions which must certainly be put to the Bible, and which will be more significant than all the pedantic criticism of the Bible of the nineteenth century.

When we come to the fourth post-Atlantean epoch, we can say of it: Now there is present a body in which Christ can incarnate. It was not there in the preceding epochs; but now it is there. In this fourth epoch, however, humans lack the possibility of finding their way to a real understanding of what is happening. Indeed a strange paradox, is it not? For the fact that confronts us is actually this: Christ appeared on Earth in an epoch that was least adapted to understanding Him. And when we look at all the attempts that were made in subsequent centuries to understand the nature of Jesus Christ, we find endless theological wrangling. Finally in the Middle Ages a sharp distinction is drawn between knowledge and faith—which implies a complete abandonment of any knowledge about the being of Jesus Christ ... not to speak of modern times, which up to the present have remained powerless in face of this manifestation.

A truly remarkable phenomenon! Christ was born in the very epoch that was least adapted to understanding Him. And if in the evolution of humanity the essential thing had been for Christ to work on the *understanding* of human souls on Earth, then—one must say it—this working would have been in a sad way. One might perhaps call that putting it very strongly; but in order not to be misunderstood I want to say this: To anyone who looks from the standpoint of anthroposophy at the history of theology in relation to the Christ-Event, it must seem as though theology had deliberately set out to place one hindrance after another in the way of understanding Christ. For theological erudition seems to take a course that leads it farther and farther away from this understanding. That is rather radically expressed, but anyone ready to enter into this way of putting it will be able to grasp the deeper meaning of my words.

Now, fundamentally speaking, it is certainly not easy to unravel the riddle I have been speaking of, and I avow that in the course of time I have tried to come near it through the most varied ways of spiritual research. Obviously there is not time to speak of these ways now. But there is one way among the many that I should like to mention. It is the way that leads round at the beginning of our era through a very remarkable manifestation of spiritual life—the life of the sibyls.

These sibyls were indeed a remarkable phenomenon, with a prophetic character entirely their own. External scholarship cannot even say from which language the word 'sibyl' comes. As soon as we start looking at the fairly detailed knowledge about the sibyls that external documents provide, we come upon something quite extraordinary, at the very beginning of the sibylline age. From about the eighth century BCE onwards we encounter the first abode of the sibyls, in Ionian Erythrae; from there the first sibyls sent out into the world their manifold prophecies. And these prophecies, even in the form handed down by external tradition, show that they arose from strange subconscious regions of human nature and the life of the soul. As though out of chaotic, psychic depths the sibyls utter all kinds of prophecies about the future development of this or that people, telling mainly of awful things to come, but sometimes also of good things. Far removed from anything like orderly thought, the utterances of the sibyls pour out in such a way that—if they are studied with the means of anthroposophy—it seems as one listens that every sibyl is a spiritual fanatic who wants to force upon people what she has to say. She does not wait to be questioned, in the manner of the Greek Pythian[18] oracle; she steps forth, the people assemble, and her utterances about peoples and evolutionary cycles seem to ring out with overbearing force.

It is remarkable, as I said, that the sibyls should appear first in Ionia, for Ionia was at the same time the birthplace of Greek philosophy: the wisdom which from Thales[19] and Aristotle[20] on into the Roman epoch is so pre-eminently an expression of a well-ordered life of soul, entirely opposed to anything chaotic. It draws forth from the life of the soul all that can be expressed in clear, lucid, light-filled concepts. From Ionia sprang the philosophy of clarity and light, which with Plato—one might say—became the philosophy of the heavenly. And like its shadow appear the sibyls, with their psychic products emanating from the chaos of the soul, often shedding a true illumination on the future, but also often announcing things which their followers had to falsify in order to make it seem that the prophecy had been fulfilled.

And then we see further how the sibyls, always accompanying the fourth cultural epoch like a shadow of its wisdom, spread through Greece, through Italy. We hear tell of the most varied kinds of sibyls, and we see sibyllism spreading on through Italy, until we come to the time of the Mystery of Golgotha. Then we see how sibyllism gains influence over the Roman poets; how it even plays into the poems of Virgil[21]; how it is just the intellectuals who try to shape their lives by appealing to the sayings of the sibyls. How much importance was attached to these sayings is shown by the so-called Sibylline Books,[22] which were consulted for guidance. And again in the external world we see how in connection with the sibylline sayings great intelligence is chaotically mixed up with arrant humbug. And then we see sibyllism even gaining a foothold in Christianity. We hear its voice in Thomas of Celano's hymn:

Dies irae, dies illa,
solvet saeclum in favilla,
teste David cum Sibylla.[23]

And so, right into the time of the development of Christianity, many minds were aware of the sibyls and their prophecies, especially those that bore on doom and destruction and the coming of a new order of the world. Hence one can say that through many, many centuries—indeed all through the fourth post-Atlantean epoch and with an influence extending, if only sparsely, into the fifth epoch[24]—the sibyls are encountered in the history of humanity. Only someone dominated by present-day rationalistic ideas can overlook the far-reaching influence of sibyllism on the world in which Christianity grew up. As I have often said, the history we are given to read is in many respects a *fable convenue*,[25] especially where anything of a spiritual nature is concerned. Until quite recent centuries, the ideas of all classes of people were influenced much more widely than is generally believed by what came from the sibyls. Sibyllism is a remarkable, enigmatic phenomenon, occurring as it did in the fourth post-Atlantean epoch.

What really went on in the souls of the sibyls must be of interest to us, for through spiritual research we have to unearth such things from beneath the layer of materialistic culture which covers them nowadays. In this condition they are useless; they must be brought to light and renewed by the resources of spiritual research which are available in our epoch. But attention must also be drawn to the fact that in comparatively recent times the nature of sibyllism was not forgotten to the extent it is today. We have indeed an important work of art which points to the traditions concerning the significance of sibyllism. Perhaps we do not always look at this work with an awareness of its significance in this respect, but the significance exists and should give occasion for reflection. I mean the great paintings in the Sistine Chapel, where Michelangelo[26] depicted not only the development of Earth and humanity, but also the Prophets and the sibyls. And in looking at these paintings we ought to notice the way in which Michelangelo portrays the sibyls, and particularly how he contrasts them with the Prophets. In this contrast, if we look at it impartially, we find something that through anthroposophy we can recognize as having to do with various hidden aspects of the fourth post-Atlantean epoch, during which the Mystery of Golgotha was fulfilled.

In this wonderful work of art we see first the portrayal of the Prophets—Zechariah, Joel, Isaiah, Ezekiel, Daniel, Jeremiah, Jonah. And ranged with them are the sibyls—the Persian, Delphic, Erythraean, Libyan, and Cumaean sibyls. Almost all the Prophets, we find, have to a greater or lesser degree something of the character which strikes us immediately in Jeremiah and comes out with particular significance in Zechariah: they are deeply reflective men, for the most part absorbed in books or something similar, quietly taking into well-ordered minds whatever it is they are studying. In the countenances of these Prophets we encounter the calmness of their souls. Daniel looks like a slight exception, but only an apparent one. He stands before a book that is supported on the back of a boy; he has in his hand something to write with, in order to write down in another book what he is reading. Here there is a slight effect of transition from reading the secrets of the world to writing them down; while the other Prophets remain in meditation, calm and relaxed in soul, entirely devoted to the secrets of the world. In gazing at them we see—and this must be kept firmly in mind—that they are all absorbed in supra-earthly things; their souls are at rest in the spiritual and they are seeking to fathom the emergence of humanity from out of the spiritual. We see that in their thinking they are far removed from their immediate surroundings, far above human passion and fanaticism, untouched by the ecstasy that may spring from these emotions; they are not only beyond human ken, but beyond anything humans can experience in themselves in so far as they are on Earth. That is the greatness of this portrayal of the Prophets by Michelangelo.

Michaelangelo's depiction of the Prophet Jeremiah in contrast to the Persian sibyl (Sistine Chapel)

Then we turn our gaze to his depiction of the sibyls. Here we have first the Persian sibyl, close to the Prophet Jeremiah, contrasting remarkably with his meditative demeanour. She raises her hand as though wishing to force on humanity what she has experienced; as though in the style of a bad speaker she wants to add all possible emphasis to her words; as though impelled by the passion of a fanatic to impose with imperious gesture her message on all humanity. Then we turn to the Erythraean sibyl; we see how she is connected with everything that can accrue to humans from the elemental secrets of the Earth. Above her head is a lamp; a naked boy is lighting the lamp with a torch. How could the intention of the painting be more clearly expressed? Here is human passion kindling out of the unconscious forces of the soul the message that is to be instilled with all the power of prophecy into humanity.

The Prophets are devoted in their souls to the primal eternity of the spirit; the sibyls are carried away by the earthly, in so far as the earthly reveals the psychic and spiritual. The Delphic sibyl shows this particularly clearly: we see how her hair is even blown to one side by a gust of wind, and the same wind catches her blue veil, so that she has the element of air to thank for what she imparts. In this gust of wind we see pictured what the Earth wished to reveal through the lips of this sibyl, with forcibly persuasive power. Then the Cumaean sibyl! She speaks with half-open mouth, as though muttering; as though stammering out a prophecy from the unconscious, the unknown. The Libyan sibyl, the hasty one, looks as though she is turning round to grasp something from which secrets can be read—something like that! In these sibyls everything is devoted, so to speak, to the immediate element of earth.

Much was entrusted to images of this kind in the days when—as we can readily understand—things could be much more effectively expressed in paintings and other forms of art than they would be in our time, when concepts and ideas are more to the purpose.

What then is the special character of these sibyls? What are they? What does their prophesying signify? We must penetrate deeply into the mysteries of human evolution if we want to fathom what went on in the souls of these sibyls.

With this aim in view, let us ask again: Why would it have been so easy for the old Indian rishis, with their scarcely conceivable wisdom, to understand Jesus Christ? It seems trivial, yet it is true to say—because they had the necessary concepts and gifts of wisdom, and in the fourth post-Atlantean epoch these were lacking. They had everything for which the Gnostics, and the anti-Gnostics, and the Apostolic Fathers,[27] as they are called, thirsted in vain. They had it all, but in what form did they have it? Not as ideas that had been worked out, somewhat as the ideas of Plato and Aristotle were worked out, but as inspirations, as something that stood before them with the full power of concrete inspirations. Their astral bodies were laid hold of by that which streamed into them from the great cosmos, and out of this working of the cosmos on their astral bodies came the concepts that could have conjured up before their souls the being of Jesus Christ. One might say that this was given to them. They had not worked it up for themselves; it came as though showered forth from the depth of the astral body. And with wonderful clarity it showered upon the holy rishis and their pupils, and fundamentally speaking upon the whole Indian culture of the first post-Atlantean epoch. It became more and more narrowed down, but in the second and third post-Atlantean epochs it was still there, and the remains of it passed over into the fourth epoch. But what was this remainder?

If we were to examine what things were like in the third post-Atlantean epoch, we should find that at least those who had raised themselves to the height of their epoch—and proportionately there were many more spiritually developed persons than there are today—had ideas about the interconnections of the supra-earthly and the symbolic significance of the starry heavens. They could read secrets of the world in the motions of the stars. It is quite certain that the third post-Atlantean epoch, if Christ had appeared on Earth then, would have known from the writing in the stars what relationship it had with Him. But—in accordance with the principle we have often mentioned with regard to the evolution of humanity—it was necessary that the gift of entering into relation with the mysteries of the world through living pictures should recede more and more into the background of human astrality. These pictures became increasingly chaotic. What flowed by this channel into the human soul became less and less authoritative—I am not saying that it lost all authority—but it became less and less authoritative as a means of fathoming the real mysteries of the cosmos.

And so two quite different developments can be traced. On the one hand, there was the world of concepts, let us say of Plato and Aristotle; a world of ideas which could be called the most attenuated form of the spiritual world, a world which had in it the least of spirit, a world grasped and explored directly by the ego and no longer experienced through the astral body. For that is the distinguishing mark of Greek philosophy: there for the first time the spirit spoke out of the ego, as it can do, in concepts that were perfectly lucid, but far removed from real spiritual life. But the Greek philosopher still felt that his thoughts emanated from the spiritual world, whereas modern philosophers are by necessity doubters, sceptics, because they no longer feel any connection between their thoughts and the mysteries of the world. In modern times, there has been a decline in the faculty for saying: When I think, the spirit of the world is thinking in me.

As I have tried to show in *The Threshold of the Spiritual World*,[28] it is necessary to gain, through meditation, a little of that confidence in the forming of concepts and ideas which came naturally to the Greek philosophers, because they were able to accept their thoughts as thoughts of the spirit of the world itself. Only the outermost fringe of the spirit of the world approached humanity through Greek philosophy, but it was a fringe permeated with the actual life of the spirit of the world; and this was felt to be so.

The second element that persisted from older times was atavistic, an heirloom, and it persisted most plainly in the prophecies of the sibyls. Out of the chaos of their inner life, they brought forth once more the human psychic forces which had worked harmoniously during the second and third post-Atlantean epochs, and now gave confused glimpses of the spiritual world.

Let us take a hypothesis that in our present context is perhaps permissible: What would have happened if neither the Christ nor Greek philosophy had come into the world? Humanity would then have had to get along with what it had received as inheritance from the past, and in the fourth post-Atlantean epoch this had reached the stage of sibyllism. Imagine this developing on its own lines in the West, without the Christ-Impulse and without philosophy, and without the science that rests upon philosophy—then you will have a picture of the spiritual chaos that would have overtaken the West, arising inevitably from all that had been active in the souls of the sibyls. But forces have after-effects. If one examines with the resources of anthroposophy this elemental strength, through which the spiritual powers connected with wind and water and fire find expression in the immediate circumference of the Earth, and if one studies how these powers would have found an abode in human souls—especially if one tests the strength with which the spirits of wind and fire, water and earth, would have taken possession of human souls—then one can see how harmony and order had faded out of the old way of knowing the world, prevalent during the first three post-Atlantean epochs, and how the forces only would have remained in human souls.

Human souls would have lost the capacity for relating themselves truly to the great phenomena of the cosmos, but they would have assuredly had a relation with the spirits of wind and water, fire and earth, and particularly with the whole tribe of spectres and demons which would have got loose from their cosmic connections. Humans would have fallen quite under the sway of the elemental spirits; their teachers would have been of the sibylline kind, and the force would have been so strong that it would have persisted right up to the present, and indeed up to the very end of earthly days. And if we ask why this has not happened, and who has brought it about that the force so apparent in the sibyls has gradually declined, then we must answer: Christ, who through the Mystery of Golgotha infused the Earth's aura with His Being; thus He destroyed the sibylline force in human souls and has driven it away.

And so on the ground of anthroposophy we observe the remarkable fact that human wisdom has not understood much about the Christ-Impulse; our concepts and ideas have turned out to be virtually powerless in this respect. But the essential thing is not that the Christ-Impulse came into the world primarily as a teaching. The essential thing is the character of the facts, the direct impulse that flowed from the Mystery of Golgotha. And this we must look for not only in what is taught or understood, but in what is accomplished for human souls. And one of these deeds, the struggle waged by Christ, who had permeated the aura of the Earth, against sibyllism—it is this deed that I wished to bring before you today.

Thus the Christ had in fact to fulfil the office of a judge. This was misunderstood by those who took it materialistically to imply that Christ would return soon after His resurrection. Human concepts at that time could not reach to an understanding of these things. But in the chaotic ideas of an early return there was the truth that there had been this early manifestation of Christ. He had manifested on ground that (as we shall see tomorrow) had been prepared externally by Paul; but above all He had manifested in the region behind the sensory world where the spiritual conflict between Christ and the sibyls had been waged. We must pierce the veil that shows us the spreading of Christianity on the physical plane. We must look behind the physical plane at the spiritual conflict whereby human souls were freed from that chaotic element which would otherwise have gone on from strength to strength. And this fact is seen in a false light by anyone who fails to comprehend that through this supra-physical deed something of endless value was accomplished for humanity by Christ.

But who were they who achieved at least something, indeed much, towards this comprehension? They were the writers of the Gospels, and Paul, who were endowed with a certain inspiration or revelation from the spiritual world.

We shall have to appreciate from other points of view the emergence of the Evangelists and of Paul. But we can now see how Paul stands in the midst of a world where something is going on beyond the reach of his words, beyond all that he could contribute through his powerful, fiery words towards an understanding of the Mystery of Golgotha. And yet—particularly if one grasps the nature of the struggle waged by the Christ against the sibyls—one has a feeling about Paul that I would like to sum up in a few concluding words. With Paul it always seems that there is much more between his words than one gets from simply reading them. It is as though the vision of Damascus had come to expression through him; as though there penetrated into humanity through him a note which was opposed to the prophetic note of the sibyls; as though through him there rang out again the note of the old Prophets whom Michelangelo has represented so beautifully in his paintings. As I have said, the sibyls had something that came from the elementals of the earth; something that could not have been there if the elemental spirits of the earth had not spoken to them. With Paul there was something similar, something which external scholarship has noted in a remarkable but quite exoteric way; and this, if one examines it from the standpoint of anthroposophy, really leaves one standing before a world of amazement.

Paul also, in a certain way, created something out of the elemental nature of the Earth, but in a distinctive region of the Earth. Naturally one can understand Paul quite well in a theological, rationalistic, abstract way if one leaves out of account what I am going to say, for this cannot be explained in terms of external science. One can understand Paul quite well, if one wants to understand him only from the standpoint of ordinary rationalism. But if one wants to grasp what it was that lived spiritually in Paul, in and between his words, and why one feels through his words something akin to the prophecies of the sibyls, but with him proceeding from a good element in Earth evolution, then one comes to the phenomenon which answers the question: How far does Paul's world extend? What are its boundaries? And the remarkable answer we receive is: Paul is great throughout the world where the olive tree is cultivated. I know I am saying something strange, but we shall see that this strangeness explains itself, in a certain sense, when tomorrow we enter a little into the character of Paul.

Geographically, too, the world is full of secrets. And the region of the Earth where the olive tree flourishes is different from the regions where flourish the oak or the ash. As physically embodied beings, we have a relationship with the elemental spirits. In the world of the olive tree the rustle and movement, the whisper and gesture, are not the same as in the world of the oak or the ash or the yew. And if we want to grasp the connection of Earth's nature with human beings, we need to pay attention to such peculiar facts as this—the fact that Paul carries his message just as far over the Earth as the domain of the olive tree extends. The world of Paul is the world of the olive tree.

Lecture 3

LEIPZIG, 30 DECEMBER 1913

THESE lectures are so arranged that separate themes will be introduced, and then I shall bring in considerations that will lead towards the themes and throw light upon them. One theme, accordingly, resides in what was said about the difficulty of understanding the being of Jesus Christ. Then we came to the symptom of the prophecies of the sibyls as illustrating one side of human psychic life during the fourth post-Atlantean epoch. Finally, at the close of yesterday's lecture, I introduced the theme of Paul and the olive tree.

I will return to these leading themes, but we must approach them, as it were, in circles, with our themes inscribed at the centre. What is really meant by the themes will then gradually emerge. Today I would like to say something about the being of Christ as such. We shall then see how in Paul the being of Christ is reflected in a certain definite way.

From earlier lectures we know that the being of Christ can be understood if we follow the evolution of our system back to the Ancient Sun existence.[29] And on various occasions, in lectures already published, attention has been drawn to the fact that in the being of Christ we have to do with a high spiritual being—that is the term we will use for the present—for whose own evolution the Ancient Sun period was especially important. I will not go further into that just now. We will simply look up to the being of Christ as a high spiritual being. But for understanding human evolution something else is necessary, and we have seen how necessary it is, for in relation to a certain fact the concepts and ideas that in the fourth post-Atlantean epoch aspired to understand the being of Christ were powerless to do so.

Again and again, especially during the early centuries among the Gnostics, among the Apostolic Fathers, and among the persons who contributed in one way or another to the founding of Christianity, this question came up: How was the nature of Christ related to the nature of Jesus? Now we already know that we have to distinguish two Jesus-boys. Of one of these we need not speak further here, for he can be readily understood from previous anthroposophical explanations. I mean the Jesus in whom lived the Ego of Zarathustra. Here we have a human being who in the second post-Atlantean epoch had already reached a high degree of evolution; who at that time founded the Zarathustrian spiritual stream and then had subsequent lives; who later reincarnated in the Solomon Jesus-child and in him, up to his twelfth year, underwent the development appropriate for so lofty an Ego in that period. We know also that Zarathustra's ego passed over into the body of the other Jesus-child, on whose nature the Gospel of Luke throws some gleams of light.

We must now consider a little this Nathan Jesus-child. I have already drawn your attention to the fact that in this child we have not to do with a human being, like other human beings, in the strict sense of the term. We cannot say of this being that he had previously been incarnated on Earth in this or that individual. We have always emphasized that of the element of soul which has come forth from spiritual worlds in order to live in single individuals on Earth, something, as it were, remained behind; and that what had thus remained behind appeared in the Nathan Jesus-child. Hence of this child we cannot say that in him there lived an ordinary human ego which had developed in a certain way through earlier incarnations. We have to recognize (this follows from what is said in my book, *Esoteric Science*[30]) that he had not previously walked the Earth as man. The only question is: Did this being, whom we will now call simply Jesus of Nazareth, have any previous connection with earthly evolution?[31] We must remember that the beings and powers connected with human evolution are not confined to those who incarnate on the Earth itself; there are also spiritual beings and powers who belong to the higher Hierarchies.[32] If therefore we say that something of the substance which divided itself among single human souls remained behind, and was then in a certain sense born in the Nathan Jesus-child, we are not saying that this being had no previous relation with earthly evolution. We are saying only that he was not related to the evolution of the Earth and of humanity in such a way as to have walked the Earth as man. We must look for him not in the history of the physical Earth, but in pre-earthly spiritual realms. And then, for the kind of observation I have often spoken about—clairvoyant observation—the following is revealed.

Let us recall what is described in *Esoteric Science*—how from the Lemurian Age onwards souls gradually came down from the other planets (with the exception of one principal human pair who had stayed on Earth) and were incarnated in human bodies throughout Atlantean times. We must accordingly think of earthly evolution as being such that the souls withdrew from the Earth's cosmic surroundings and at various points of time took up again their evolution on Earth. We know that before the Lemurian Age they had gone away to other planets. But we know also that the evolution of the Earth had been exposed to the attacks of Lucifer, and later to those of Ahriman.[33] Thus human souls had to enter into bodies wherein they were exposed in the course of human evolution to the attacks of both these spiritual beings. If nothing further had come about—if, that is, the human souls had come down from planetary existence into evolution on Earth, there to encounter the luciferic and ahrimanic influences—then something else would have happened to them as they went through subsequent incarnations; something I did not intimate in *Esoteric Science*, for at the present day one cannot say everything in public.

First of all, when the human beings came down from the planets into physical bodies, the development of their senses would have been exposed to a certain danger. We must not think it was a quite simple matter for these human souls to come down from their planetary abodes and assume bodies on Earth, and that after that everything went on normally. Because the luciferic and ahrimanic principles held sway in these bodies, they were not so organized as to enable human beings to pursue the course of evolution that they did in fact pursue. If these souls had simply gone on using the forces which governed the sensory organs of these bodies, they would have had to use their senses in a peculiar way—a way not really human.

For example, the eye would have been so impressed and affected by a colour that it would have felt itself permeated with intense feeling. At the sight of one colour it would have positively glowed with pleasure; for another colour it would have felt intense, painful antipathy. And so, because of the luciferic and ahrimanic influences, the souls descending from the planets would have found no bodies equipped with senses of the right kind. They would have been tormented by sympathy and antipathy; on seeing one colour or another they would have been seized with bliss or repulsed with acute pain, all through their lives. That was how evolution was going; cosmic forces, especially those from the Sun, would have worked on the Earth in such a way as to give the senses this character. Any contemplation of the world, in a spirit of quiet wisdom, would have been ruled out. So a change had to be brought about in the forces which flowed from the cosmic environment into the Earth and had built up the human senses. In the spiritual world, something had to happen so that these forces would not turn the senses into mere organs of sympathy and antipathy, for they would then have been under the sway of Lucifer and Ahriman. Hence the following took place.

The being of whom we have said that he had not chosen the path down from the planets to the Earth, but had remained behind, the being who later appeared as the Nathan Jesus-child and who had dwelt from primal ages in the spiritual worlds—this being resolved (if we may use this expression, for of course all these expressions are taken from human speech and cannot fully convey what one wants to say) while still in the world of the higher Hierarchies to go through a development which would enable him to be permeated for a time by the being of Christ. Thus we have to do not with a man but with a supra-human being who (if we may speak in this way) lived in the spiritual world and, as it were, heard the distress of the human sensory system crying out to the spiritual world for help, and in response to this cry made himself fitted to be permeated by the Christ.

So it was that in the spiritual worlds the being who later became the Nathan Jesus-child was permeated by the being of Christ, and then brought about a change in the cosmic forces which were streaming in to build up the human senses. These senses were changed in such a way that instead of being mere organs of sympathy and antipathy, they became organs that human beings could use, and so could look with wisdom at all the nuances of sensory perception. Very differently would the cosmic forces have flowed into humanity if this event, far back in the Lemurian Age, had not taken place in the spiritual worlds. This being who appeared as the Nathan Jesus-child then still dwelt (if I may use the phrase) in the sphere of the Sun, and because he listened to the human cry of distress, he experienced something which made it possible for him to be permeated by the very Spirit of the Sun, so that the activity of the Sun was lessened in such a way that the human sense organs, which derive essentially from solar activity, did not become organs of mere sympathy and antipathy.

Here we touch upon a significant cosmic secret, and one which will enable us to understand much that happened later on. A certain order and harmony, imbued with wisdom, could now flow into the realm of the human senses, and evolution could go on normally for a while. The worst activity of Lucifer and Ahriman had been turned away from the human senses by a deed in the higher worlds.

Later on came a time, in the Atlantean Age, when it once more became apparent that the human bodily constitution could not be a suitable instrument for the further course of evolution. The human vital organs, and their underlying forces in the etheric body, which for a time had developed in a suitably useful way, had fallen into disorder. For the cosmic forces which had worked on them from the surroundings of the Earth, and whose task it was to bring order into these organs—the organs of breathing, blood circulation and so on—these forces would have developed under the influence of Lucifer and Ahriman in such a way that the vital organs would have ceased to be usable by human beings on Earth. They would have acquired a quite peculiar character. The forces that provide for these vital organs do not flow in directly from the Sun, but from the seven planets, as they used to be called. The planetary forces worked from the cosmos into humanity. And it was necessary that these forces, also, should be modified. If they had remained under the sway of Lucifer and Ahriman, the vital organs would have become merely organs of greed or organs of loathing. For example, people would not have been able to restrain themselves from hurling themselves greedily upon a given dish, while a terrible loathing would have driven them from another. These are things that unveil themselves as world secrets, as cosmic secrets, when we try to penetrate into them clairvoyantly.

So again something had to happen in the spiritual worlds themselves in order that this destructive activity should not enter into human life. And this same being, who later appeared as the Nathan Jesus-child and who (as we have explained) dwelt in earlier times on the Sun and was there permeated by the being of Christ, the sublime Spirit of the Sun—this being went from planet to planet, touched in his innermost nature by the fact that human evolution could go no further, as things were. And this experience affected him so strongly, while he was assuming a form of body on the different planets, that at a certain time during the Atlantean evolution the Spirit of Christ permeated him again. And through what was now brought about by the permeation of this being by the Spirit of Christ, it became possible for moderation to be implanted in the vital human organs. In the same way that wisdom had been given to the sensory organs, so moderation was now bestowed on the vital organs. Thus it came about that when people breathed in a particular place, they were not impelled to suck in the air greedily, or to recoil with loathing from the air in another place. That was the deed accomplished in the spiritual worlds through a further permeation of the Nathan Jesus-child by the being of Christ, the high Spirit of the Sun.

Then in the further course of human evolution a third thing happened. A third confusion would have arisen if the souls had been obliged to continue using the bodies then available for them on Earth. We can put it in the following way.

At this time the physical nature of humanity was essentially in order. Through the two deeds of Christ in the supra-sensory world, the human sense organs were in a condition serviceable for us on Earth, and so were the vital organs. But it was not so with the organs of the soul: thinking, feeling, and willing. If nothing further had happened, these organs of the soul would have become disordered. I mean that willing would have been continually disturbed by thinking, feeling would have interfered with willing, and so on. Humans would have been condemned, as it were, to a perpetually chaotic use of these organs of the soul. They would have been maddened by an excess of will, or confused by repressed feeling, or there would have been people plagued with fleeting ideas through a hypertrophy of thinking, and so forth. This was the third great danger to which humanity was exposed on Earth.

Now these three faculties of the soul, thinking, feeling and willing, are coordinated from the surroundings of the Earth, for the Earth itself is essentially the scene of action for the ego. The working together of thinking, feeling, and willing has to be kept in order; not, however, from all the planets, but only from Sun, Moon, and Earth, so that through the interworking of Sun, Moon, and Earth, if this is harmonious, humans are made fit for the harmonious cooperation of these three faculties.

Help for these faculties of the soul had to be provided from the spiritual world. And now the soul of that being who later became the Nathan Jesus-child assumed a cosmic form such that his life was in a sense neither on the Moon nor on the Sun, but as though it encircled the Earth and felt a dependence on the influences of Sun, Moon, and Earth at the same time. The earthly influences came to him from below; the solar and lunar influences from above. Clairvoyant observation really sees this being, in the springtime of his evolution—if I may use that phrase—in the same sphere as that in which the Moon goes round the Earth. Hence I cannot say exactly that the lunar influence came to him from above, but rather that it came to him from the place where he was, this pre-earthly Jesus-Being. Again there rose to him a cry of distress, a cry that told of what human thinking, feeling, and willing were on the way to becoming; and he sought to experience completely in his own inner being this tragedy of human evolution. Thereby he called to himself the high Spirit of the Sun, who now for the third time descended upon him, permeating him. So in the cosmic height, beyond the Earth, there was a third permeation of this Nathan Jesus-child by the high Spirit of the Sun whom we call the Christ.

Now I would wish to depict for you this third ensouling rather differently from the way in which I described the other two. What took place through three successive stages of spiritual evolution—or heavenly evolution, I would say—was reflected in the various world outlooks of the post-Atlantean peoples. For it had effects which worked on into later times; the Sun's activity continued to be influenced by the fact that in ancient Lemurian times the being who afterwards became the Nathan Jesus-child had been permeated by the being of Christ. And the essential thing about the initiation of Zarathustra was that he perceived the activity of the Sun impregnated with this influence. In this way Zarathustra's teaching arose; his initiation had revealed to him—had projected into his soul—what had happened in primeval times.

The third post-Atlantean epoch, which we call the Egyptian-Chaldean epoch, came about partly through the reflection in human souls, as a continuing human experience, of the activities that had originated from the permeation of the Nathan Jesus by the Spirit of the Sun while that being was journeying round the planets. From this arose that science of planetary activities which comes before us in Chaldean astrology; people today have a very meagre conception of what it really was. Among the Egyptian-Chaldean peoples of the epoch there developed also that star worship which is indeed known exoterically; it arose because the moderating of planetary influence was still making itself felt at that later time.

Later still, in the fourth post-Atlantean epoch, we can see in Hellenism a reflection of planetary spirits who had, as it were, come into existence because the being who had been permeated by the Christ journeyed from planet to planet and on each planet became one or other of these spirits. On Jupiter, he became the one whom the Greeks later called Zeus; on Mars, the one later called Ares; on Mercury, the one later called Hermes. In the Greek planetary gods, there was this later reflection of what Christ in the supra-sensory worlds had made of the planetary beings who were imbued with the luciferic and ahrimanic principles. When a Greek looked up to his heaven of the gods, he came into touch with the adumbrations, the reflections, of the activity of Jesus Christ on the individual planets, together with much else that I have described.

To this was added as a third event the reflection or adumbration of that which the being of Jesus, in the later post-Atlantean times, had experienced as a celestial being in relation to Sun, Moon, and Earth. If we are to characterize this we can say: The Christ 'ensouled' himself in an angelic being. We say of Christ that he *embodied* himself in Jesus of Nazareth, but we are speaking now of an event that took place in spiritual worlds: the Christ 'ensouled' himself in an angelic being. And the effect was that human thinking, feeling, and willing took an orderly course. This was an important event, coming early in the evolution of humanity: the development of the human faculties of the soul was brought into good order. The two earlier Christ-events had brought order rather into the bodily constitution of humans on Earth. What then had had to happen in the celestial worlds for this third event to come about?

It will be easier to recognize this third event if we look for the reflection of it in Greek mythology. For just as the planetary spirits projected themselves into the figures of Zeus, Ares, Hermes, Venus or Aphrodite, Kronos and so on, so was this third cosmic event reflected not only in Greek mythology, but also in the mythologies of the most diverse peoples. We can understand how it was reflected if we allow ourselves to compare the reflected images with their sources; if, that is, we compare what happened in Greece with what first happened in the cosmos.

What was it that happened up there in the cosmos? The need was to drive out something that would have raged chaotically in human souls; this had to be overcome. The angelic being who was permeated with the Christ had to accomplish the deed of vanquishing and driving out from the human soul that which had to be driven out if thinking, feeling, and willing were to be harmonized. And so there arises the picture—let us bring it vividly before our souls—of an angelic being, dwelling still in the spiritual worlds, who later became the Nathan Jesus-child: he appears to us ensouled by the Christ and thereby rendered capable of special deeds—able to drive out from thinking, feeling, and willing the element which would have raged within them as a dragon and brought them into chaos.

A reminiscence of this is preserved in all the pictures of St George vanquishing the dragon that are found in the records of human culture. St George and the dragon reflect that celestial event when the Christ ensouled the being of Jesus and enabled him to drive the dragon out of the human soul. This was a significant deed, made possible only with the help of Christ in the being of Jesus, at that time an angelic being. For this angelic being had actually to connect himself with the nature of the dragon; to take on, as it were, the form of the dragon in order to hold off the dragon from the human soul. He had to work from within the dragon, so that the dragon was ennobled and brought out of chaos into a kind of harmony. The training, the *taming* of the dragon—that is the further task of this being. And so it came about that the dragon indeed remained active, but because there was poured into him the influence and power of the being I have described, he became the bearer of many revelations which proved their worth to human civilizations throughout the course of post-Atlantean evolution. Instead of the chaos of the dragon manifesting in maddened or bewildered human beings, the primal wisdom of the post-Atlantean time came forth. Jesus Christ used the dragon's blood, as it were, so that with His help it could transfuse human blood and thereby make human beings the vehicles of divine wisdom. A significant reflection of this is apparent—even quite exoterically—in Greek mythology from the ninth century BCE onwards.

It is remarkable how for the Greek mind one particular divine figure emerged from the others. The Greeks, we know, reverenced a variety of gods. These gods were the reflections or projections of the beings who originated from the journey round the planets of that being, permeated by the Christ, who later became the Nathan Jesus-child. The Greeks saw them in such a way that when they looked out into cosmic spaces, when they looked up through the light-ether, they rightly ascribed to the planet Jupiter—in an inward spiritual, not an external, sense—the origin of the being they spoke of as Zeus. So they spoke of Pallas Athene, of Artemis, of the various planetary gods who were the reflections of what we have spoken about.

But from these pictures of the various figures of the gods there emerged one figure—the figure of Apollo. The figure of Apollo emerged in a distinctive way. What did these Greeks see in him?

We come to know Apollo if we look at Parnassus and the Castalian spring. To the west of it there was a cleft in the Earth, and over this the Greeks built a temple—why? Vapours used to rise up out of the cleft, and when the currents of air were right, the vapours crept up the mountainside like the coils of a snake, like a dragon. And the Greeks imagined Apollo as shooting his arrows at the dragon, as it rose from the cleft in the form of turbulent vapours. Here, in the Greek Apollo, we see an earthly reflection of St George, shooting his arrows at the dragon. And when Apollo had overcome the dragon, the Python, a temple was built, and instead of the dragon we see how the vapours entered into the soul of the Pythia, and how the Greeks imagined that Apollo lived in these swirling dragon-vapours and prophesied to them through the oracle, through the lips of the Pythia. And the Greeks, that self-conscious people, rose through the stages for which their souls had been prepared; they accepted what Apollo had to say to them through the Pythia, who was imbued with the dragon-vapours. It meant that Apollo lived in the dragon's blood and filled humans with wisdom from the Castalian spring. And this became a meeting-place for the most sacred plays and festivals.

Why was Apollo able to do this—who was he? It was only from spring to autumn that he caused wisdom to flow up from the dragon's blood. Towards autumn, he went away to his ancient home in the north, in the Hyperborean land. Farewell festivals were held at the time of his departure, and his return was welcomed in the spring. A deep wisdom resides in this idea of Apollo going north. The physical Sun withdraws towards the south; in a spiritual sense it is always the opposite. The story shows that Apollo has to do with the Sun. Apollo is the angelic being of whom we have spoken; he was a reflection, projected into the Greek mind, of the angelic being who had in fact worked at the end of the Atlantean time and who had been permeated by the Christ. This reflection was the Apollo who spoke wisdom to the Greeks through the mouth of the Pythia. And what was the content for the Greeks of this Apollo wisdom? We might say it was everything that led them, on the most important occasions, to take this or that decision. Again and again people went to Apollo at difficult moments in their lives, with their souls well prepared, and received prophetic guidance from the Pythia, who was stimulated by the vapours in which Apollo lived. And Asklepios, the healer, is for the Greeks the son of Apollo, the healing god. The weakened form of the Angel in whom Christ once dwelt is a healer on Earth, or for the Earth. For Apollo was never physically embodied, but he worked through the elements of Earth.

And the god of the Muses, above all the god of song and the art of music, is Apollo. Why is this? Because through the power of song and string music he brings thinking, feeling, and willing into harmony. We have only to keep firmly in mind that in Apollo there was a projection of what had happened at the end of the Atlantean time. Something had then worked from spiritual heights into the human soul, and a weak echo of it could be heard in the musical art cultivated by the Greeks under the protection of Apollo. They knew it as an earthly reflection of the ancient art which the angelic being, permeated by the Christ, had cultivated in the heavenly heights in order to bring thinking, feeling, and willing into harmony. They did not say so openly; only in the Mysteries was the meaning of it understood.

In the Apollonian Mysteries, it was said: A high, divine being once sank himself into a being of the Hierarchy of Angels, and thereby brought harmony into thinking, feeling, and willing. The art of music was a reflection of that happening, especially the Apollonian art that flowed from the sound of strings. The music which demands less of the elements than wind instruments do; which depends in the main only on the skill of human hands; in short, the music that sounds from the strings of Apollo—to this music the Greeks ascribed the musical effects which bring harmony into the soul. And persons who have no inclination for Apollo's music, or do not value it highly enough, were said by the Greeks to carry a bodily mark of their obtuseness in this respect; a sign that they had stayed behind, atavistically, at an earlier stage.

It is remarkable that when a certain man—King Midas—was born with exceptionally long ears, the Greeks said he had come into the world with ass's ears because in his life before birth he had not rightly devoted himself to the influence of the being whom the Christ had ensouled. Therefore, said the Greeks, he had ass's ears, and that was why he preferred wind instruments to string instruments. And when once a child was born who, so to speak, had no skin—he is known in mythology as the Flayed Marsyas—the Greeks said it was because before his birth he had not paid heed to all that flowed from the angelic being. For that is how it looks to esoteric observation: Marsyas was not flayed in his lifetime, but before his birth, and it was then that his misdeed occurred.

Many towns founded by the Greeks as colonies were named Apollonia, because the sites for them had been chosen after consulting the Pythia. The Greeks cherished their freedom and so were not politically united, but they had an ideal unity through the god Apollo, for whom a kind of confederation was founded later on.

We see how the Greeks revered in the god they called Apollo the being of whom we have spoken; and we might say that in the being who truly corresponded to Apollo at the end of the Atlantean time, the Christ was ensouled. Who then was Apollo—not the reflection revered by the Greeks, but Apollo himself? A celestial being who from the higher worlds poured out healing forces for the soul, paralysing the luciferic and ahrimanic powers. These forces brought about in the human body a harmonious cooperation of brain, breath, and lungs with the larynx and the heart, and it was this that came to expression in song. For the right cooperation of brain and breathing with the speech organ and the heart is the bodily expression of harmony in thinking, feeling, and willing. The healer, the celestial healer, is Apollo. We have seen this being pass through three stages of evolution, and then the healer, whom Apollo reflected, was born on Earth and he was called Jesus, which in our language means 'He who heals through God'. He is the Nathan Jesus-child, the one who heals through God, Yehoshua-Jesus.[34]

Now, at this fourth stage, this being made himself ripe to be ensouled with the being of Christ, with the 'I'. This came to pass through the Mystery of Golgotha. For if this Mystery had not been enacted—if the being whom we have followed through cosmic ages had not given embodiment to the Christ—then in the course of later time, human souls would not have found bodies in which the force of the ego could come to necessary expression on Earth. The ego had been brought to its highest stage in Zarathustra. The souls who had taken part in the evolution of the ego would never have found earthly bodies suitable for its further development if the Mystery of Golgotha had not come to pass.

We have now seen the four stages of harmonization: the harmonizing of sense perception, of the life-organs, of thinking, feeling, and willing, and the harmonization in the ego, this last through the Mystery of Golgotha. You have the connections between the being who was born as the Nathan Jesus-child and the being of Christ, and the way in which this was prepared. It is now possible, through that which it is permissible to reveal in true anthroposophy, to understand this kind of growing together, belonging together, of the being of Christ and the human nature of Jesus. This is possible for us. And a healthy development of spiritual life in the future will depend on this—on it becoming possible for more and more people to grasp that which could not be grasped by the thoughts and ideas of the epoch in which the Mystery of Golgotha was fulfilled.

Lecture 4

LEIPZIG, 31 DECEMBER 1913

YESTERDAY we spoke of how preparation was made for what had to come about for the evolution of humanity through the Mystery of Golgotha. We spoke of the three permeations of a being of the higher Hierarchies by the Christ, and in the wonderful emergence of the Greek Apollo we found an echo of what had taken place at the end of the Atlantean time, as a far distant prefiguring of the Mystery of Golgotha. Now we have to inquire how the effects of this are manifest in the evolution of humanity. It will first be necessary to say something about the basic characteristics of the worldviews that appeared in post-Atlantean times as the echoes, or after-effects, of the threefold Christ-event, for this, as we have seen, reached a certain conclusion at the end of the Atlantean age.

Let us try to look more deeply into the fundamental characteristics of these worldviews. They arose as after-effects in human souls of all that I described yesterday. These post-Atlantean worldviews are indeed the reflections of the threefold Christ-event in the souls of post-Atlantean humanity. From this point of view, we need say only a few words about the first post-Atlantean epoch. We have often characterized it from other points of view. We know that in terms of spirituality it was the highest post-Atlantean epoch up to now, but that what the souls of the holy rishis and their disciples received from it was less penetrated by the Mysteries of which I spoke yesterday.

The first post-Atlantean worldview to show a direct effect of the threefold Christ-event was that which arose from the Zarathustrian impulse. Now I must here remark in parenthesis that I shall have to introduce words which—because of the way they are used today—have a dry, abstract, even pedantic sound; but, search as one may through the language there are no other words available. And so I shall want to appeal to your souls to understand by these words something far more spiritual than anything they can signify for the dry scholarship of the present time.

From the point of view relevant here I should like to associate the Zarathustrian worldview with 'chronology'. It looks beyond the two beings, Ahura Mazdo[35] and Ahriman, to the workings of Time—Zurvan Akarana.[36] Not, however, the abstract Time we think of today, but Time viewed as a living, supra-personal being. From this being proceed the rulers of Time; first of all the Amshaspands, the spiritual beings who are symbolized in cosmic space by the signs of the Zodiac. Through the number six—or twelve if we reckon in their antipodes—they rule over the Izeds, who rank below them and are 28–31 in number. The Izeds are spirits of a lower kind, servants of the high Time-beings; they regulate the days of the month.

The Zarathustrian consciousness looked at the wonderful harmony that works through forces and is symbolized numerically by all the relations and combinations which result from the interweaving of 28 to 31 with 12. It looked into all that streams into the world and resounds through it, because in the great world-orchestra the instruments sound harmoniously together in these numerical relationships. For the Zarathustrian worldview this appears as the ordering and harmonizing principle in the cosmic order. I want to give only a hint of these relationships. And because in what creates, and nourishes itself in creating, in what takes the worldview into itself, absorbing them spiritually and carrying them over to higher stages—because the Zarathustrian outlook sees in 'Time' something living and supra-personal—so, while spiritualizing the term, we may call this worldview 'chronology', whereby we are led to think at once of the god Kronos, the Regent of Time.

Then we come to the third post-Atlantean epoch. Yesterday I described it as the epoch in which knowledge was kindled in human souls by the forces that shone out from the stars; when the secrets of the world were no longer discerned only through the relations between the Rulers of Time in the supra-sensory, for these were becoming manifest in the realm of sensory existence. In the courses of the stars, in the signature of their movements in cosmic space, humans could now perceive how harmony and melody in cosmic happenings are brought about. This worldview I would like to call astrology. So chronology is followed by astrology. And everything that was disclosed by the true, authentic chronology of Zarathustrianism, and by the true, authentic astrology of the Egyptian and Chaldean Mysteries—all this was activated by the secret influence that had come into the world through the threefold Christ-event before the Atlantean catastrophe.

And what followed in Greece or in the Graeco-Latin epoch? What I am now going to say applies not only to the Greek and Roman cultures, but also to all the other regions of Europe. Yesterday I tried to illustrate it through a single example, but it holds good, one might say, for all the West. Let us recall how the Greeks reverenced Apollo, the reflection of the Nathan Jesus-child as he had been at the end of the Atlantean time. It was out of the Hyperborean land, from the North, that Apollo came to the Oracle at Delphi. Through the Pythia, in summer, he spoke the most important things that the Greeks wished to hear. In the autumn, he returned to his Hyperborean land. We connected this journey of Apollo with the journeys of the Sun; but it is the *spiritual* Sun that speaks through Apollo, and the spiritual Sun goes away to the north, while the physical Sun goes to the south. The myths are seen to be endlessly filled with wisdom if they are considered in the light of true esotericism. But in revering Apollo, the Greeks did not look on the Sun as his visible sign in the heavens; Apollo was not a solar god in this sense. For a god symbolized by the external Sun the Greeks had Helios; it was he who regulated the course of the Sun in the sky. Even if we take only the physical Sun into account, we find that its influence on earthly life is not confined to the direct effects of its rays. The Sun works in the first place through air and water and water-vapour, and so through the vapours which (as we have seen) rise from the site of the Castalian spring and coil round the neighbouring hillsides like a dragon—the dragon killed by the Greek St George. The Sun works in all the elements, and after it has worked into them, inoculated them, its activity plays out from them on to human beings through the servants whom we call elemental spirits. In the elements, the Spirit of the Sun is actively alive, and this is the activity the Greeks saw in their Apollo.

Thus for the Greeks, Apollo was a solar god, but not the Helios who drove the chariot of the Sun across the heavens and to some extent regulated the times of the day. In Apollo, the Greeks saw the Sun's activity in the atmosphere, and this activity they addressed as Apollo when they addressed it spiritually. And so it was with many gods and spiritual beings whom we find in the West. I could mention many, but we need point only to Wotan with his wild host, rushing through the storm. What form then did the worldview—still echoing the threefold Christ-event—take in the fourth post-Atlantean epoch? Again I must make use of a pedantic, dried-out word. Astrology was followed by meteorology. Chronology, astrology, meteorology! We have only to bring the 'logy' into relation with the Logos.

But while all this was breaking in over the Western world, something else streamed into the whole post-Atlantean civilization. This too was an after-echo of the threefold Christ-event, but it came from quite another side. And this fourth element, running as though parallel to the meteorology of the fourth post-Atlantean epoch, is something I must again designate with a dry, pedantic word: geology—but I beg you once more to relate the 'logy' to the Logos. Geology, then—where do we encounter it?

The development of the ancient Hebrew civilization will never reveal its particular secrets unless it is studied as geology, in our sense of the term. How do we first come upon the ranks of the Elohim, or upon the Yahweh-god?[37] We meet him first when he wishes to form into the human something taken from the Earth itself. He wishes to clothe with a new covering, an Earth-vesture, the part of the human being that has come down from earlier times, from Saturn, Sun, Moon. Yahweh is precisely the god who forms humans out of the Earth—that is, out of the forces and elements of the Earth. Therefore, the ancient Hebrew wisdom, since it professed the Yahweh-god, had to become geology. And this teaching about humans, that they are formed out of the forces of the Earth, is geology. Is not the geological character of the ancient Hebrew teaching shown to us at once in the name of the first human, Adam—he who was formed out of Earth! That is the significant point that we must keep before us: among other peoples—the peoples with a meteorological world-picture, let us say—the creation of humans is spoken of quite differently, with the emphasis on their souls. In the Greek worldview, for example, we see Prometheus engaged in the forming of the human being. Athena lends her aid and causes a spark from spiritual heights to be united with humanity. Prometheus forms the soul in the symbolic likeness of a butterfly. The God Yahweh forms the human being out of Earth; and he, Yahweh, having become in the course of his evolution the Ruler of Earth, breathes out of his own substance a living soul into humans. So Yahweh unites himself through his breath with what he has formed out of Earth. And he wishes to dwell in his offspring, in his living breath, in Adam and his descendants; those beings whom Yahweh considered it his task to clothe in Earth. And now to carry this further, let us try to call up before our souls everything we find handed down by the Bible from Hebrew antiquity itself.

We know, and have emphasized, that the Earth develops certain forces. Goethe[38] and Giordano Bruno,[39] among others, compare these forces to those of in-breathing and out-breathing in human beings. The Earth does have forces of inhalation and exhalation that bring about ebb and flow, the swelling and sinking of the waters; they are inner forces of the Earth, but the same as those which guide the Moon round the Earth. In the effects of water we encounter a manifestation of these forces of the Earth. In this realm, the Bible shows us the Deluge as another important event after the creation of Adam, the 'man of Earth'. And now let us pass on to the time of Moses!

If we look at the actions of Moses in the right light, we find them constantly related to activities of the Earth. Moses goes to the rocks with his rod and makes water gush out. Moses goes up the mountain. Above and below, the mountain is connected with the Earth's activity. For we must think of this mountain as a volcano, or at least as volcanic. It is not the Sinai generally imagined; the Earth is active in it. The column of fire in which Moses stands is akin to what happens when we burn a piece of paper in the sulphurous hills of Italy and smoke comes out. So does fiery smoke, telluric activity, come out of the mountain. And in telluric activity the Jews always saw symbols. In front of them went the pillar of cloud or of fire—telluric activity! We could go deeply into details and everywhere we should find that the Spirit of Earth prevails in all that Moses gives out as a revelation of Yahweh. What Moses proclaims is geology!

The profound difference between the Greek and the Hebrew worldviews will never be understood unless it is recognized that the Greek conception belongs to meteorology, and the Hebrew conception to geology. The Greeks felt that they were living in the midst of forces pouring in on the Earth from the surrounding cosmos; pouring into the air and pervading the atmosphere. The Hebrews felt themselves in close relationship to forces rising from the Earth below and bound up with the Earth. Yes, even the sufferings of the Hebrew people come from the desert, where the forces of the Earth prevail. Geology dominates the destiny of the Hebrews. Geology, expressed now in the fruitfulness of the Earth, is what draws them, through the reports of their scouts, to the Promised Land.[40]

Paul knew well that this consciousness of a connection with the Spirit of the Earth is a result of the pre-earthly Christ-event, for he indicates that it was the Christ who led the Jews through the desert and caused water to flow from the rock. And if we were to go on from the Bible to some of the significant Hebrew legends, we should find them permeated with geology, in the sense meant here. Thus we are told how Yahweh, when he was forming humans out of Earth, sent forth an Angel to gather Earths of different colours from all parts of the Earth, so that everything belonging to the Earth should be mingled in Adam's bodily vesture. Today we should say that Yahweh took great care to place humans on the Earth so that in our true being we would be the highest flower, the crown, of earthly creation.

For the Chaldeans, the Egyptians, the Zoroastrians, the Greeks, the Romans, and the European peoples of Central and Northern Europe, the most important part of the human being was the part that came from the spiritual world. For the Jews, the most important element in the human being was connected with the Earth and its forces. Yahweh felt himself as the god whose spiritual rulership prevailed throughout the Earth.

Thus we can regard as the most important event in the fourth post-Atlantean epoch the emergence of geology side by side with meteorology. And a wonderful spiritual reflection of this comes to expression in ancient Hebrew prophecy.

What were these Prophets really striving for? Let us try to look into the prophetic souls of Isaiah, Jeremiah, Hezekiah, Daniel, Joel, Jonah, and Zechariah. If we do this quite impartially, without any preconceptions, we find that they were endeavouring, fundamentally, to bring a particular faculty into the forefront of the soul and to drive another faculty down, as it were, into the depths. I have already asked you to notice how, in the paintings by Michelangelo which I described, the Prophets are always depicted sitting there as if wrapped in deep thought, inwardly at rest, so that one sees how in the devotion of their souls they are connected through subearthly depths with the eternal. In contrast with them, Michelangelo places the sibyls, who are open to the elemental powers of the Earth. Thus, the hair of one sibyl is blown about by the wind; even her blue mantle billows in the wind, and under the influence of the wind she utters her prophecies. We see another sibyl seized by inner fire; in the typically assertive gesture of her hand we see the fire, the earthly element. We could look again at these sibyls one by one and we should find that they live in the midst of the forces that play into their souls from the elemental surroundings of the Earth. These sibylline forces, which, so to speak, draw into their souls the spirit of the elements and bring it to expression—these are the forces that the old Jewish Prophets wanted to repress. If you read impartially the whole history of the Jewish Prophets, you will find that the Prophet sets himself—and that is the aim of his training—to suppress in himself the sibylline urge and to prevent it from ever breaking out.

Apollo changed the sibylline impulse of the Pythia by sinking himself into it and speaking through her. The Prophets wanted to suppress everything Pythian in their souls and to cultivate solely what works in the clear force of the ego; the ego which is bound up with the Earth and belongs to it; the ego which is the spiritual counterpart of the geological element. How the Eternal reveals itself in the ego through calm repose, when the sibylline elements are silent, when all inner turmoil ceases, when only calm prevails and gazes into the grounds of the eternal—that is what the Jewish Prophets wished to manifest, so that their proclamations could spring from a temper of soul which corresponds in the highest degree with geology.

Thus the stirring message that sounds forth to us from the Prophets is like an outflowing of the geological element, and even when things turn out quite differently from what has been prophesied, this very fact shows us how closely bound are the Prophets to the element of geology. A future kingdom which will redeem the existing kingdom while remaining in all appearance an earthly kingdom, a heaven on Earth—that is first of all what the Prophets announce, so closely are they united with geology.

This geological element in the Prophets flowed on even into the early days of Christianity, since people expected not only the return of the Messiah, but that he would come down from the clouds and found his kingdom on Earth. The distinctive inner character of Jewish culture will be understood only if it is taken in this sense as geology. This was what the Prophets longed for and inculcated in their pupils—to suppress the sibylline element, together with everything that leads the soul into unconscious depths, and to make manifest that which lives in the ego.

The relations of all other peoples to their gods were different from those of the Jews to Yahweh. The other relations were predetermined: they reflected the outcome of the relations of humans to the spirits of the higher Hierarchies during the Saturn, Sun, and Moon periods. The Jewish people had the task of developing a relationship that belonged specially to the period of Earth. But when the ego wishes to establish a relationship with its god, how does this find expression? Not as inspiration, so that morality springs from the operation of divine forces within the soul, but as *commandment*. The form of commandment found in the Decalogue is encountered first among the Jews—whatever nonsense learned people may talk about earlier commandments, Hammurabi,[41] and so forth. I cannot go now into the follies of modern scholarship. The commandments that arise when the ego stands directly over against God and receives from God the rule, the precept, that the ego must follow out of its own inner will—this kind of commandment is met with first among the Jewish people. And it is here, too, that we first find God entering into a covenant with his people.

The other gods worked with forces that are always connected with subconscious realms of the soul. Let us recall how Apollo worked through the Pythia, and how a person on his way to the Pythia had to prepare himself, so that the god might be able to speak to him. Apollo spoke through the unconscious psychic life of the Pythia. In contrast with this, we have Yahweh uttering his commandments, making a covenant with his people, speaking directly to the ego in the soul. And the Prophets immediately waxed wrath if something happened which did often happen to the Jewish people—if the influence of heathen peoples gained sway over the Jews. No subconscious forces were to be allowed to influence the Jews; everything had to rest on the alliance with God and the principle of the Law. That was the especial concern of the Prophets. And now let us look back a little, with the aid of esoteric knowledge, over what we have already tried to illustrate.

Yesterday we came to know about the threefold Christ-event that took place in Lemurian and Atlantean times. We saw how on three occasions the being who appeared later as the Nathan Jesus-child was permeated by the Christ, but in such a way that he did not incarnate on Earth but remained in spiritual worlds. And when we look back over what happened then, we must say that what was accomplished in Atlantean times flowed over into the East.

For example, Elijah was one of the Prophets—but in what sense is he a Prophet? He is a servant of the God Yahweh, but in his soul an echo of the threefold Christ-event lives on. In his soul is the knowledge: 'As a Prophet of Yahweh, I must above all things proclaim that in Yahweh there lives the Christ who will later on fulfil the Mystery of Golgotha; the Christ who poured His enduring influence into the cosmos through His third experience at the end of the Atlantean time.' Elijah proclaimed the Christ-filled Yahweh. For the Christ was indeed living in Yahweh, the God Yahweh, but as a reflection of Himself. As the Moon reflects the sunlight, so did Yahweh reflect the being who then lived as Christ. Christ caused His being to be reflected from Yahweh or the God Yahweh. But a messenger such as Elijah worked in the after-effects of the threefold Christ-event; we might say that Elijah went ahead of the Nathan Jesus, Who was passing spiritually from West to East in order to find His way into the course of civilization and then to be born as one of the Jesus-children.

The overflow, as it were, of meteorology, especially when this came into touch with geology, was felt by all peoples as a heralding of things to come. And we meet with the remarkable fact that in the region which afterwards became so important for Christianity, one of these prefiguring signs occurred. We see how in the most varied places of Asia Minor, and also in Europe, festivals were held which were like foreshadowings of the Mystery of Golgotha. The cults of Attis[42] and Adonis[43] have been correctly noted as having this character. But if we look at these festivals in their true light, we see that the event they prefigure is on the meteorological level. The god who was slain as Adonis, and who rose again, was not thought of as embodied in the flesh. What his worshippers had for a god was primarily an image, a picture; and in fact it was a picture of the angelic being who in spiritual heights was permeated by the Christ at the close of the Atlantean time and was later born as the Nathan Jesus-child. It was the destiny of the Nathan Jesus-child that was celebrated in the worship of Adonis and Attis.

We can now say that it was part of the karma of world history—you will perhaps look for something more behind these words—that in the place where the Bible with a certain truth locates the birth of the Jesus-child—in Bethlehem—there was a centre of the Adonis cult. Bethlehem was one of the places where Adonis had been worshipped. The Adonis who died and rose, again was often celebrated there, and so was an aura prepared by the calling up of a memory: Once in the spiritual heights there was a being who then belonged still to the Hierarchy of Angels and was later to come to Earth as the Nathan Jesus-child; a being who at the end of the Atlantean time had been permeated by the Christ. What had formerly been done for the harmonizing of thinking, feeling, and willing—this was celebrated at the Adonis festivals. And in Bethlehem, where Adonis festivals had been held, we have also the birthplace of the Nathan Jesus-child. In conjunction, these words sound strange. But when we have sought out the threefold Christ-event, the supra-earthly event which on three occasions preceded the Mystery of Golgotha, do we not see the Christ pass over from West to East, to the place where the Mystery of Golgotha was to be fulfilled? Do we not see how He had sent His messenger in Elijah, and do we not know how in his next incarnation the messenger reappeared as John the Baptist?[44] And are we not expressly told of this in a wonderful harmony of words: 'He sent his angel before him, to herald his coming'? That can be said as well of John as of Elijah. Or even better of Elijah, as will be understood by those who remember my saying that Elijah remained in spiritual heights and worked through a representative, so that he himself never went about on Earth. If you reflect on that, the expression, 'He sent his angel before him', is even more appropriate to Elijah than to John. Such messengers were always messengers of the Christ, who was passing from West to East.

And now the geology of the Jews was to be permeated by the spiritual being whom we have learnt to see as having a particular activity in relation to the Earth. Geology was to be Christened [*durchchristet*]. The Spirit of the Earth was to be experienced in a new way by humans; they had to be enabled to free this spirit, in a certain sense, from the Earth. But this was possible only if there came a power which could free the Spirit of the Earth from the forces of the Earth. This happened when the Earth's aura was permeated by the power of the Christ and in consequence a change came over the Earth itself. The Christ entered into the forces that the God Yahweh had released and gave them a different character.

From all this, if we look back over it, we can understand why the laurel became a visible symbol of Apollo. For those who bring something of anthroposophy to the study of the plant kingdom, the laurel has a strong connection with meteorological conditions. It is shaped and built out of meteorology. Another plant is much more closely bound up with the Earth; is so to speak an expression of geology. If one really feels how the oil penetrates the olive tree, so that in one's own soul the elemental forces are stirred by the way in which the tree allows a new sprout to be grafted on to it and to flourish there—then one can feel how the olive tree is inwardly penetrated with the oil of Earth. One can feel the earthly element pulsing through the oil.

And now you will remember something I touched on in the second lecture—that Paul was called to build a bridge between Hebrew antiquity and Christianity, between geology and Christology. As we said, Paul's activity extends through the realm of the olive tree. And if we understand Apollo in the vapours rising from the mountain chasms, and how through the vapours he inspires the Pythia and speaks oracular words concerning human fate, then we can also feel how the elemental forces stream from the olive tree into its environment, and these are forces familiar to the soul of Paul. We can feel it in his words. He immerses himself, as it were, in geology in order to feel the elemental forces in the aura of the olive tree and to let its aura inspire him in that geographical realm where his work lay.

Nowadays people read these things far too abstractly. They imagine that things said by writers in the past were as abstract, as dependent only on the brain, as are the things often said by modern authors. People do not reflect how not only understanding and reason, but all the forces of the soul, can be connected in a primordial earthly sense with all that gives a certain region its particular stamp. It was the olive tree that gave its stamp to the Pauline region. And when Paul sought to raise the Jewish geology up to himself, inspired by the olive tree—he spoke the most important things concerning the relationship of the Christ-filled human being to humans who are far from Christ. Let us hear the strange words Paul uses when he wishes to bring the Gentile Christians into relation with the Jews. They are not to be taken abstractly, but as words that rise new-minted from the elemental depths of his soul:

> But I have something to say to you Gentiles. I am a missionary to the Gentiles, and as such I give all honour to that ministry when I

> try to stir emulation in the men of my own race, and so to save some of them. For if their rejection has meant the reconciliation of the world, what will their acceptance mean? Nothing less than life from the dead! If the first portion of dough is consecrated, so is the whole lump. If the root is consecrated, so are the branches. But if some of the branches have been lopped off, and you, a wild olive, have been grafted in among them, and have come to share the same root and sap as the olive, do not make yourself superior to the branches. If you do so, remember that it is not you who sustain the root: the root sustains you.
>
> You will say, 'Branches were lopped off so that I might be grafted in'. Very well: they were lopped off for lack of faith, and by faith you hold your place. Put away your pride, and be on your guard; for if God did not spare the native branches, no more will he spare you. Observe the kindness and the severity of God—severity to those who fell away, divine kindness to you, if only you remain within its scope; otherwise you too will be cut off, whereas they, if they do not continue faithless, will be grafted in; for it is in God's power to graft them in again. For if you were cut from your native wild olive and against all nature grafted into the cultivated olive, how much more readily will they, the natural olive-branches, be grafted into their native stock! [Romans XI 13–24]

Thus wrote he of whom tomorrow we will speak further, showing how he took what he had to say from Jewish geology and drew a superb picture of the elemental forces which rise up from the Earth and reign in the olive tree.

LECTURE 5

LEIPZIG, 1 JANUARY 1914

I HAVE spoken to you about the sibyls, pointing out how they appear as shadows of the Greek philosophers in Ionia. Through centuries they conjured up from their chaotic souls a mixture of deep wisdom and sheer spiritual chaos, and they exerted much more influence on the spiritual life of Southern Europe and its neighbouring regions than external history is willing to recognize. I wanted to indicate that this peculiar outpouring from the souls of the sibyls points to a certain power of the human soul which in ancient times, and even in the third post-Atlantean epoch, had some good significance. But as one cultural epoch succeeds another in the course of human history, changes occur. The forces that the sibyls employed to produce, at times, sheer nonsense, were good, legitimate forces in the third post-Atlantean epoch, when astrology was studied and the wisdom of the stars worked into human souls, harmonizing the forces which later emerged chaotically as sibyllism.

You can gather from this that forces which prevail anywhere in the world—including those which prevailed in the souls of the sibyls—should never be called good or bad in themselves; it depends on when and where they appear. The forces that appeared in the souls of the sibyls were good and legitimate, but they were not adapted to the fourth post-Atlantean epoch; for the forces that were then intended to prevail in human souls were not those that come from subconscious depths, but those that speak to the soul through the clarity of the ego. Yesterday we heard how the Hebrew Prophets strove to suppress the sibylline forces and to bring out the forces that speak through the clarity of the ego. This indeed was the essential characteristic of the old Hebrew school of prophecy—to press back the chaotic sibylline forces and to bring out those that can speak through the ego.

The fulfilment of this task given to the Hebrew Prophets—we could call it a task of bringing the sibylline forces into the right path of evolution—came about through the Christ-Impulse. When the Christ-Impulse entered into the evolution of humanity in the way known to us, one result was that the chaotic forces of the sibyls were thrust back for a time, as when a stream disappears below ground and reappears later on. These forces were indeed to reappear in another form, a form purified by the Christ-Impulse, after the Christ-Impulse had entered into the aura of the Earth. Just as in human life, after we have been using our psychic faculties throughout the day, we have to let them sink into nightly unconsciousness, so that they may reawaken in the morning, so it was necessary that the sibylline forces, legitimate as they had been during the third post-Atlantean epoch, should flow for a while below the surface, unnoticed, in order to reappear—slowly, as we shall hear.

The forces—legitimate human forces—which emerged so chaotically in the sibyls were cleansed, so to speak, by the Christ-Impulse, but then they sank below the surface of the soul. Human beings in their ordinary consciousness remained entirely unaware that the Christ continued to work on these forces; but so it was.

From the standpoint of anthroposophy, it is a superb drama to watch this impact of the Christ-Impulse; to see how, from the Council of Nicaea[45] onwards, human beings in their normal consciousness quarrel ardently about dogmas, while what was most important for Christianity takes its course in the subconscious depths of the soul. The Christ-Impulse does not work where there is strife, but below the surface, and human wisdom will have to uncover a great deal that we may think strange if we look at it superficially. Much will have to be revealed as a symptom of the Christ-Impulse working below the surface. Then we shall understand that essential developments in the historical configuration of Christianity in the West could not come about through the quarrels of bishops, but sprang from decisions which were reached below the surface of the soul and rose into consciousness like dreams, so that people were aware only of these dreamlike apprehensions and could not puzzle out what was going on in the depths. I will mention only one symptom of this. There are events that reflect, as though through dreams, the activity which the Christ was undertaking in the depths of the soul in order to bring the human forces of the soul into a right alignment with the course of Western history.

Many of you will perhaps guess something of what I mean if we observe that on 28 October, 312, when Constantine the Great,[46] the son of Constantine Chlorus, was making war against Maxentius on the outskirts of Rome, a decision was taken which proved to be of the highest importance for the configuration of Christianity throughout the West. This battle in front of Rome was not determined by military orders, or by the conscious acumen of the leaders, but by dreams and sibylline omens! We are told—and this is the significant thing—that when Constantine was moving against the gates of Rome, Maxentius had a dream which said to him: 'Do not remain in the place where you are now.' Under the influence of this dream, reinforced by an appeal to the Sibylline Books, Maxentius committed the greatest folly—looked at externally—that he could have committed. He left Rome and fought the battle—with an army four times the size of Constantine's—not within the protection of the walls of Rome, but outside them. For the message received from the Sibylline Books ran thus: 'If you fight against Constantine outside the gates of Rome, you will destroy Rome's greatest enemy.' A truly oracular utterance! Maxentius obeyed it and with faith and courage went outside the gates. As on an earlier occasion another sibylline oracle had guided Croesus,[47] so was Maxentius guided by this one. He destroyed the enemy of Rome—himself.

Constantine had a different dream. It said to him: 'Carry in front of your troops the monogram of Christ!' He did so and he won the battle. A decisive event for the configuration of Europe, brought about by dreams and sibylline sayings! There we gain a glimpse of what was going on below the surface in the souls of Europeans. Truly, like a stream that has disappeared into mountain cavities, so that it is no longer to be seen up above and one may form the strangest conjectures about it, so the Christ-Impulse works on below the surface—works, at first, as an esoteric, i.e. hidden, reality.

My dear friends, allow me at this point to confess to you that when in my esoteric researches I tried to follow this stream, I often lost trace of it; I had to search for places where it reappeared. I could suppose that the stream of the Christ-Impulse had reappeared slowly, and that even today it has not fully reappeared but can only give evidence of itself. But where and how did it come to the surface? That is the question. Where did it lay hold of souls sufficiently to make an impression on their consciousness?

If you follow up the various expositions in my books and courses of lectures, and if you feel about it as I do, you will find, especially in the older ones, that what I have said in connection with the name of the Holy Grail is one of the least satisfying parts. That is how I feel and I hope that others have felt it, too. It is not that I have said anything that could not be upheld, but simply that when I spoke of this, I felt unsatisfied. I had to give out what could be told with confidence, but often, when I tried to trace the further course of this stream—when I tried to unravel the further esoteric development of Christianity in the West—then before my soul rose the admonition: 'You must first read the name of Parsifal in its right place.'

I had to experience the fact that esoteric researches are guided in a remarkable way. So that we may not be enticed into speculation, or into realms where we can very easily be borne away from esoteric truth on the wings of fantasy, we have to be guided slowly and by stages, if at last our research is to bring to light the truth which can of itself impart a kind of conviction of its rightness. So I often had to be content with waiting for an answer to the injunction: 'Search out where the name of Parsifal stands!' I had quite understood something you all know from the Parsifal saga—after Parsifal returns, in a certain sense cured of his errors, and again finds the way to the Holy Grail, he is told that his name will appear shining upon the Holy Vessel. But where is the Holy Vessel—where is it to be found? That was the question.

In esoteric researches of this kind one is often held back, delayed, so that one may not do too much in a day or a year and be driven on to speculate about the truth. Landmarks appear. For me they appeared in the course of really a good many years, during which

I sought an answer to the question: Where will you find the name of Parsifal written on the Holy Grail?

I knew that many meanings can be attached to the Holy Vessel in which the Host, the holy bread or wafer, is placed. And on the Holy Vessel itself 'Parsifal' was to shine. I was aware also of the deep significance of a passage such as that in St Mark's Gospel, Chapter 4, verses 11 and 12, 33 and 34, where we are told that the Lord often spoke in parables and only gradually clarified their meaning. In esoteric investigation, too, one is led gradually, step by step, and very often only in connection with karmic guidance, and on encountering something that seems to have to do with a certain matter, one very often does not know what will be made of it in one's own soul under the influence of forces coming from the spiritual world. Often one does not know in the least whether something drawn from the depths of the esoteric world will have a bearing on some problem that one has been following up for years. Thus I did not know how to proceed when I once asked the Norwegian Folk Spirit, the Northern Folk Spirit, about Parsifal and he said: 'Learn to understand the saying that through *my* powers there flowed into the northern Parsifal saga *Ganganda greida*'—'circulating viaticum', or something like that![48] I had no idea what to make of this. It was the same when I was coming out of St Peter's in Rome under the strong impression made on me by Michelangelo's work that you find on the right-hand side as you enter—the Mother with Jesus, the Mother who looks so young, with Jesus dead already on her knees. And under the after-effect of looking at this work of art (this was a guidance of the kind I mean), there came to me, not as a vision but as a true Imagination from the spiritual world, a picture which is inscribed in the Akashic Record,[49] showing how Parsifal, after he has gone away for the first time from the Castle of the Grail, where he had failed to ask about the mysteries which prevail there, meets in the forest a young woman who is holding her bridegroom in her lap and weeping over him. But I knew that whether it is the mother or the bride whose bridegroom is dead (Christ is often called the Bridegroom), the picture had a meaning, and that the connection thus established—without my having done anything about it—had a meaning also.

I could tell you of many indications of this kind that came to me during my search for an answer to the question: Where can I find the name of Parsifal inscribed on the Holy Grail? For it had to be there, as the saga itself tells us; and now we need to recall the most important features of the saga.

We know that Parsifal's mother, Herzeleide, bore him in great suffering and with dreamlike visions of a quite peculiar character; we know that she wished to shield him from knightly exercises and the code of knightly virtue; that she arranged for the management of her property and withdrew into solitude. She wanted to bring up her child so that he would remain a stranger to the impulses that were certainly present in him; for he was not to be exposed to the dangers that had surrounded his father. But we know also that from an early age the child began to notice everything glorious in nature; from his mother's teaching he really learnt nothing except that there was a ruling God, and he conceived a wish to serve this God. But he knew nothing of what this God was, and when one day he met some knights he took them for God and knelt before them. When he confessed to his mother that he had seen the knights and wanted to be a knight himself, she put on him a fool's garments and sent him forth. He met with many adventures, and later on—people may call this sentimental but it is of the deepest significance—the mother died of a broken heart because of her son's disappearance: he had not turned back to give her any farewell greeting but had gone forth to experience knightly adventures.

We know that after many wanderings, during which he learnt much about knightly ways and knightly honour, and distinguished himself, he came to the Castle of the Grail. On other occasions, I have mentioned that the best literary account of Parsifal's arrival at the Castle is to be found in Chrétien de Troyes.[50] There we are shown how, after often mistaking the way, Parsifal comes to a lonely place and finds two men: one is steering a little boat and the other is fishing from it. They direct him to the Fisher-King, and presently he encounters the Fisher-King in the Grail Castle. The Fisher-King is old and feeble and has to rest on a couch.

While conversing with Parsifal, the Fisher-King hands him a sword, a gift from his niece. Then there appears first in the room a page carrying a spear; the spear is bleeding and the blood runs down over the page's hand; and then a maiden with the Holy Grail, which is a kind of dish. But such glory streams forth from it that all the lights in the hall are outshone by the light of the Holy Grail, just as the stars are overpowered by the light of Sun and Moon. And then we learn how in the Holy Grail there is something with which the Fisher-King's aged father is nourished in a separate room. He has no need of the sumptuously appointed meal of which the Fisher-King and Parsifal partake. These two nourish themselves with earthly food. But each time a new course—as we should say nowadays—is served, the Holy Grail withdraws into the room of the Fisher-King's aged father, whose only nourishment comes from what is within the Holy Grail.

Parsifal, to whom it had been intimated on his way from Gurnemanz that he ought not to ask too many questions, does not inquire why the lance bleeds or what the Vessel of the Grail signifies—naturally he did not know their names. He then goes to bed for the night, in the same room (according to Chrétien de Troyes) where all this has happened. He was intending to ask questions in the morning, but when morning came he found the whole castle empty—nobody was there. He called out for someone—nobody was there. He got dressed, and downstairs he found his horse ready. He thought the whole company had ridden out to hunt and wanted to ride after them in order to ask about the miracle of the Grail. But when he was crossing the drawbridge it rose up so quickly that his horse had to make a leap in order not to be thrown into the castle's moat. And he found no trace of the company he had encountered in the castle on the previous day.

Then Chrétien de Troyes tells us how Parsifal rides on and in a lonely part of the wood comes upon a woman with her husband on her knees, and weeping for him. It is she, according to Chrétien de Troyes, who first indicates to him how he should have asked questions, so as to experience the effect of his questions on the great mysteries that had been shown to him. We then hear that he went on, often wandering from the right road, until exactly on a Good Friday he came to a hermit, named Trevricent. The hermit tells him how he is being cursed because he has wasted the opportunity of bringing about something like a redemption for the Fisher-King by asking questions about the miracles in the castle. And then he is given many and various teachings.

Now when I tried to accompany Parsifal to the hermit, a saying was disclosed to me—a saying which in the words I have to use for it, in accordance with anthroposophical investigation, is nowhere recorded—but I am able to give you the full truth of it. It was spoken—and it made a deep impression on me—by the old hermit to Parsifal, after he had made him acquainted, as far as he could, with the Mystery of Golgotha, of which Parsifal knew little, although he had arrived there on a Good Friday. The old hermit then uttered this saying (I shall use words that are current among us today and are perfectly faithful to the sense of the utterance): 'Think of what happened on the occasion of the Mystery of Golgotha! Raise your eyes to the Christ hanging on the Cross, at the moment when He said, "From this hour on, there is your mother"; and John left her not. But you'—said the old hermit to Parsifal—'you have left your mother, Herzeleide. It was on your account that she passed from this world.'

The complete connection was not understood by Parsifal, but the words were spoken with the spiritual intention that they should work in his soul as a picture, so that from this picture of John, who did not forsake his mother, he might discern the karmic debt he had incurred by his having deserted his own mother. This was to produce an after-effect in his soul.

We hear then that Parsifal stayed a short while longer with the hermit and then set out again to find the Holy Grail. And it so happens that he finds the Grail shortly or directly before the death of old Amfortas, the Fisher-King. Then it is that the Knights of the Holy Grail, the Knights of that holy Order, come to him with the words: 'Thy name shines in the Grail! Thou art the future Ruler, the King of the Grail, for thy name shines out from the holy Vessel!' Parsifal becomes the Grail King. And so the name, Parsifal, stands on the holy, gold-gleaming Vessel, in which is the Host. It stands there.

And now, as my concern was to find the Vessel, I was at first misled by a certain circumstance. In esoteric research—I say this in all humility, with no wish to make an arrogant claim—it has always seemed to me necessary, when a serious problem is involved, to take account not only of what is given directly from esoteric sources, but also of what external research has brought to light. And in following up a problem it seems to me specially good to make a really conscientious study of what external scholarship has to say, so that one keeps one's feet on the Earth and does not get lost in cloud-cuckoo-land. But in the present instance it was exoteric scholarship (this was some time ago) that led me astray. For I gathered from it that when Wolfram von Eschenbach began to write his Parsifal poem, he had—according to his own statement—made use of Chrétien de Troyes and of a certain Kyot. External research has never been able to trace this Kyot and regards him as having been invented by Wolfram von Eschenbach, as though Wolfram von Eschenbach had wanted to attribute to a further source his own extensive additions to Chrétien de Troyes. Exoteric learning is prepared to admit, at most, that Kyot was a copyist of the works of Chrétien de Troyes, and that Wolfram von Eschenbach had put the whole thing together in a rather fanciful way.

So you see in what direction external research goes. It is bound to draw one away, more or less, from the path that leads to Kyot. At the same time, when I had been to a certain extent led astray by external research, something else was borne in upon me (this was another of the karmic readings). I have often spoken of it—in my book *Esoteric Science* and in courses of lectures—and should now like to put it as follows.

The first three post-Atlantean epochs, which occur before the Mystery of Golgotha, reappear in a certain sense after the fourth epoch, so that the third epoch reappears in our epoch, the fifth; the second epoch will recur in the sixth, and the first epoch, the epoch of the holy rishis, will recur in the seventh, as I have often described. It became clearer and clearer to me—as the outcome of many years of research—that in our epoch there is really something like a resurrection of the astrology of the third epoch, but permeated now with the Christ-Impulse. Today we must search among the stars in a way different from the old ways, but the stellar script must once more become something that speaks to us. And now observe—these thoughts about a revival of the stellar script linked themselves in a remarkable way to the secret of Parsifal, so that I could no longer avoid the belief that the two were connected with each other. And then a picture rose before my soul: a picture shown to me while I was trying to accompany Parsifal in the spirit on his way back to the Grail Castle after his meeting with the hermit Trevricent. This meeting with the hermit is recounted by Chrétien de Troyes in a particularly beautiful and touching way. I should like to read you a little of this, telling how Parsifal comes to the hermit:

> He roused the steed to start
> And sighed from out his deepest heart,
> For guilt to God doth rack his breast,
> Remorseful feelings give no rest.
> With weeping comes he through the wood
> Yet halts where hermitage has stood.
> Makes ready to dismount,
> Lays weapons on the ground—
> And finds within a chapel cell
> The pious man. 'Fore him he fell
> Upon his knees in woeful plight,
> The tear that blinked before his sight
> Now rolls at last down to his chin
> As he with simple childlike mien
> Doth fold his hands together
> That he may solace gather.
> 'Hear ye my sad confession:
> Five years I bore delusion
> While without faith my life I led
> And only strove towards the bad.'
> 'Say me wherefore thou this hast done
> And pray to God that He ere long
> Will draw thee near the holy Bond.'
> 'I once by Fisher-King did stand.
> I saw the spear upon whose steel
> Hung drops of blood. I saw the Grail

Yet did forbear to put the word
What signified this blood,
This Grail, what signified—
'Twere better had I died!
Until this day indeed
My soul's in direst need.
Our Lord I thought of never more
And from His Grace I stayed afar.'
'Now tell me what thy name may be.'
'As Parsifal men speak of me.'
Then sighs the aged man with groan,
The name to him is full well-known.
'What thou unwittingly hast left undone
Has brought this sorrow as thy doom.'[51]

Then come the conversations between Parsifal and the hermit of which I have spoken already. And when I sought to accompany Parsifal in spirit during his return to the Grail, it was often as though there shone forth in the soul how he travelled by day and by night, how he devoted himself to nature by day and to the stars by night, as if the stellar script had spoken to his unconscious self and as if this was a prophecy of that which the holy company of knights who came from the Grail to meet him had said: 'Thy name shines forth in radiance from the Grail.' But Parsifal, quite clearly, did not know what to make of the message of the stars, for it remained in his unconscious being, and therefore one cannot so very well interpret it, however much one may try to immerse oneself in it through spiritual research.

Then I tried once more to get back to Kyot, and behold—a particular thing said about him by Wolfram von Eschenbach made a deep impression on me and I felt I had to relate it to the *ganganda greida*. The connection seemed inevitable. I had to relate it also to the image of the woman holding her dead bridegroom on her lap. And then, when I was not in the least looking for it, I came upon a saying by Kyot: '*er jach, ez hiez ein dinc der gral*'—'he said, a thing was called the Grail.' Now exoteric research itself tells us how Kyot came to these words—'*er jach, ez hiez ein dinc der gral*.' He acquired a book by Flegetanis in Spain—an astrological book. No doubt about it, one may say: Kyot is the man who stimulated by Flegetanis—whom he calls Flegetanis and in whom lives a certain knowledge of the stellar script—Kyot is the man who, stimulated by this revived astrology, sees the thing called the Grail. Then I knew that Kyot is not to be given up; I knew that he discloses an important clue if one is searching in the sense of anthroposophy: he at least has seen the Grail.

Where, then, is the Grail, which today must be found in such a way that the name of Parsifal stands upon it? Where can it be found? Now in the course of my researches it had been shown to me that the name—that is the first thing—must be sought for in the stellar script. And then, on a day which I must regard as specially significant for me, I was shown *where* the gold-gleaming Vessel in its reality is to be found, so that through it—through its symbolical expression in the stellar script—we are led to the secret of the Grail. And then I saw in the stellar script something that anyone can see—only they will not immediately discern the secret. For one day, while I was following with inner sight the gold-gleaming sickle of the Moon, as it appeared in the heavens, with the dark Moon like a great disc dimly visible within it ... so that with physical sight one saw the gold-gleaming Moon—*ganganda greida*, the journeying viaticum—and within it the large Host, the dark disc. This is not to be seen if one merely glances superficially at the Moon, but it is evident if one looks closely—and there, in wonderful letters of the esoteric script, was the name Parsifal!

That, to begin with, was the stellar script. For in fact, if this *reading* of the stellar script is seen in the right light, it yields for our hearts and minds something—though perhaps not all—of the Parsifal secret, the secret of the Holy Grail. What I have still to say, briefly, on this subject I will give you tomorrow.

LECTURE 6

LEIPZIG, 2 JANUARY 1914

IN the preceding lecture, I tried to present what I had to tell you about the Mystery of the Grail and its connections in such a way as to let you see how these things reveal themselves gradually to the seeker's soul. I have not withheld the various difficulties that must be gone through before what may be called the result of research is given to the soul from out of the spiritual world. Of course I know very well that if modern psychology, which remains so superficial, gets hold of such descriptions, it will bring forward all possible—or rather the most impossible—objections. And I am well aware of all the doubts that can be raised, the curious assertions about all sorts of laws and associations of ideas and subconscious images. In spite of all this—and precisely in full consciousness of it—I have for once given you this unvarnished account, because for you, as anthroposophists, it should be important to be clear that the results to which one has to come in spiritual research are to be reached only after overcoming all the things which, as I told you yesterday, stand in the way. And the final result of spiritual research, which according to the oft-mentioned law of life can very easily reveal itself as reality, is not the outcome of ideas that have been put together, as might be supposed. For these ideas are like messengers leading to the final result and have nothing to do with the result itself.

I wanted to make these preliminary remarks because the latest publications show what happens again and again when these expositions are printed as courses of lectures. They are given to people outside our movement, who then make the most senseless remarks about them and of course take pleasure in quoting from them out of context and so on. And let me also say—without the least wish to appear presumptuous—that because of our movement a time has come when someone or other may think it profitable to attack us. And we can be sure that for such a purpose any means would serve.

I have said that the stellar script is to be found in the heavens, but it is not in any sense the Grail, and it does not yield us the Grail. I have expressly emphasized—and I beg you to take this emphasis very seriously—that the *name* of the Grail is to be found through the stellar script, not the Grail itself. I have pointed to the fact that in the gold-gleaming sickle of the Moon—as any close observer can see—the dark part of the Moon emerges and is as though marked off from the bright sickle; and there, in esoteric writing, is to be found the name of Parsifal.

Now before we go further and try to interpret this sign in the heavens, I must draw your attention to an important law, an important fact. The gold-gleaming sickle becomes apparent because the physical rays of the Sun fall on the Moon. The illuminated part of the Moon shines out as the gold-gleaming vessel. Within it rests the dark Host: physically, this is the dark part not reached by the Sun's rays; spiritually, there is something else. When the rays of the Sun fall on part of the Moon and are reflected in gleaming light, something does nevertheless pass through the physical matter. This something is the spiritual element that lives in the Sun's rays. The spiritual power of the Sun is not held back and reflected, as the Sun's physical power is; it goes through; and because it is resisted by the power of the Moon, what we see at rest in the golden vessel is actually the spiritual power of the Sun. So we can say: In the dark part of the Moon we are looking at the spiritual power of the Sun. In the gold-gleaming part, the vessel, we see reflected the physical power of the Sun. The Spirit of the Sun rests in the vessel of the Sun's physical power. So in truth the Spirit of the Sun rests in the vessel of the Moon. And if we now recollect all that we have ever said about this Spirit of the Sun in relation to the Christ, then in what the Moon does physically an important symbol will be manifest. Because the Moon reflects the Sun's rays and in this way brings into being the gold-gleaming vessel, it appears to us as the bearer of the Spirit of the Sun, for the Spirit of the Sun appears within the Moon's vessel in the form of the wafer-like disc.

And let us remember that in the Parsifal saga it is emphasized that on every Good Friday, and thus during the Easter festival, the Host descends from Heaven into the Grail and is renewed; it sinks into the Grail like a rejuvenating nourishment—at the Easter festival, when Parsifal is again directed towards the Grail by the hermit; at the Easter festival, whose significance for the Grail has also been brought nearer to humanity again through Wagner's[52] *Parsifal.*

Now let us recall how in accordance with an old tradition—one of those traditions of which I spoke yesterday as having arisen from the working of the Christ-Impulse in the depths of the soul—the date of the Easter festival was established. Which is the day appointed for the Easter festival? The day when the vernal Sun, which means the Sun that is gathering strength—our symbol for the Christ—reaches the first Sunday after the full Moon. How does the vernal full Moon stand in the heavens at the Easter festival—how must it stand? It must begin, at least a little, to become a *sickle.* Something must be visible of the dark part, something of the Spirit of the Sun, Who has gained His vernal strength, must be within it. This means that, according to an ancient tradition, the picture of the Holy Grail must appear in the heavens at the Easter festival. It must be so. At the Easter festival, therefore, everyone can see this picture of the Holy Grail. According to a very ancient tradition, the date of the Easter festival is regulated with this in view.

Now let us try again to get our bearings with regard to developments that have taken their course below the surface of the soul. Yesterday we said that the force which emerged in the sibyls had to be moderated; it had to be permeated by the Christ-Impulse. And in this moderated form it had to reappear, so that it might become the bearer of spiritual culture in later times. Now let us ask: Was Perceval—as Chrétien de Troyes calls him—able to perceive in himself something of the Christ-Impulse at work in the depths of his soul?

If we look back once more at the primal character of the ancient Hebrew geology, one thing strikes us again and again. We shall grasp the spirit of this ancient Hebrew geology only if we realize that the whole of Hebrew antiquity tried with all its might to hold fast to the geological character of its revelations. I have shown in this cycle of lectures how these revelations must be looked for, and can everywhere be traced, in the activities and spiritual mobility of the Earth. The Hebrews endeavoured to keep at bay the elemental activities that derive from the stars and served to stimulate spiritually the power of the sibyls. The influence of the stars was justified in the astrology of the third post-Atlantean epoch, for humanity then retained so much of the old ancestral spirituality that when humans devoted their souls to the elements, they absorbed a good influence from the stars.

During the fourth post-Atlantean epoch, the power of the stars receded in face of the elements that surround the Earth in the atmosphere and everywhere else. The influx of the elements was felt in such a way that anyone who understood the spirit of the age, especially as the fourth epoch advanced further and further, was constrained to say to himself: 'Let us guard ourselves against the influence that plays into the elements from the stars: it produces something like the unlawful sibylline forces.' Through the Christ-Impulse having poured itself out into the Earth's aura, the sibylline forces were to be harmonized and rendered capable of again yielding justified revelations. Never willingly did the true initiates of Hebrew antiquity look to the stars when they wished for a revelation of the spirit. They had vowed themselves to Yahweh, who belongs to the evolution of the Earth and (as I have shown in *Esoteric Science*) had become a lunar god only in order to help the Earth forward.

In the lunar festivals of the Jews it was made clear that the Lord of the Earth shines down symbolically in His reflection from the Moon. 'But go no further'—that was the warning given by old Hebrew tradition to the pupil—'Go no further! Be content with what Yahweh reveals in his symbol of the Moon—go no further! The time has not yet come for drawing out of the elements anything more than is expressed in the Moon symbol. Anything more would belong to the unlawful sibylline forces.'

When all that has come over into earthly evolution from Ancient Saturn, Ancient Sun, and Ancient Moon is grasped in its natural aspect, then we find it symbolized in the ancient Hebrew tradition through Eve. Eve—the vowels are never clearly pronounced—

Eve! Add to it the sign for the divine being of Hebrew antiquity who is the ruler of earthly history, and we have a form which is quite as valid as any other—Yeve-Yahweh, the Ruler of the Earth who has his symbol in the Moon. If we bring this into conjunction with what has come over from the Ancient Moon and with its outcome for Earth evolution, we have the Ruler of the Earth united with the Earth Mother, whose powers are a result of the Ancient Moon ... Yahweh! Hence out of Hebrew antiquity there emerges this mysterious connection of the lunar forces, which have left their remains in the Moon known to astronomy and their human forces in the female element in human life. The connection of the Ruler of the Earth with the Moon-Mother is given to us in the name Yahweh.

Now I should like to bring before you two facts that will perhaps indicate how, under the influence of the Christ-Impulse, the sibylline forces have been transformed in the subconscious depths of the life of soul. I want to touch on a manifestation to which I called attention three years ago—three years almost to the day—the transformation of a sibyl under the influence of the Christ-Impulse. In the lectures printed under the title of *Occult History: Personalities and Events in the Light of Spiritual Science*,[53] I referred to the appearance of the Maid of Orleans. I pointed out how events of the greatest importance for the destiny of Europe in the subsequent era flowed from what the Maid of Orleans accomplished under the influence of her inspirations, fully permeated by the Christ-Impulse, beginning in the autumn of 1428. From external history, one can indeed learn that the destiny of Europe would have been very different if the Maid of Orleans had not appeared when she did, and only an entirely obsessed materialist, such as Anatole France,[54] can deny that something mysterious came into history at that time.

I will not repeat here what can be read in history books; anyone who has listened to these lectures can see that something like a modern sibyl emerged in the Maid of Orleans. It was the time—the fifteenth century—when the fifth post-Atlantean epoch begins; a time when the Christ-Impulse had to emerge more and more from the subconscious depths of our souls. We can see in what a gentle, tender form, imbued with the noblest qualities of the human soul, the sibylline power of the Maid of Orleans is revealed. I would like to take this opportunity of reading to you a letter written by a man who lived through these events, for it shows what an impression the sibylline power of the Maid of Orleans made on those who had a heart and feeling for it. He was a man in the entourage of the king whom the Maid of Orleans liberated. After describing her achievements, he writes:

> This and much more has the Maid brought about, and with God's help she will accomplish still greater things. The girl is of appealing beauty and manly bearing; she speaks little and shows remarkable sagacity; when she speaks, she has a pleasing, delicately feminine voice. She eats little and abstains from wine. She takes pleasure in fine horses and weapons and admires well-accoutered and noble men. To be obliged to meet and converse with large numbers of people is abhorrent to her; her tears often overflow; she loves a happy face, endures unheard of toil, and is so assiduous in the manipulation and bearing of weapons that she remains uninterruptedly for six days—day and night—in full armour. She says that the English have no right to France, and therefore—as she says—God has sent her to drive them out and conquer them, but only after previous warning. For the King she shows the deepest veneration; she says he is beloved by God, is under special protection, and will therefore be preserved. Of the Duke of Orleans, your nephew, she says that he will be delivered in a miraculous way, but only after a demand for his release has been made to the English who hold him prisoner.
>
> With that, revered Duke, I bring my report to a conclusion. Still more wonderful things are happening and have happened than I can write of or describe to you in words. While I write this, the aforesaid Maid has already gone to the neighbourhood of the city of Rheims in Champagne, whither the King has hastily set off for his anointing and crowning under God's protection. Most respected and powerful Duke and greatly honoured master! I commend myself to you in all humility, while praying the Almighty to protect you and fulfil your desires. Written at Biteromis, the 21st day of June (in the year 1429).
>
> Your humble servant *Percival*,
>
> Lord of Bonlamiulk, Counsellor and Chamberlain of the King of the French and of the Duke of Orleans, Seneschal of Berry.

So wrote a Percival to the Duke of Milan about the Maid. Anyone reading it will feel how we have here a description of a Christ-filled sibyl.

That is one thing: the other to which I wish to call your attention is also a fact from the new times that the fifth post-Atlantean epoch brought in. It is something written by a man who, one might say, was justified in feeling himself permeated with the spirit of this new epoch—so much so that what he experienced unconsciously might be expressed as follows: Yes, a time is coming when the old astrology will live again in a new form, a Christ-filled form, and then, if one can practise it properly, so that it will be permeated with the Christ-Impulse, one may venture to look up to the stars and question them about their spiritual script. Here was a man—as you will shortly see—who felt deeply that the Earth is not as modern, materialistic geology portrays it, purely physical and mineral, but a living being, endowed not merely with a body, as the modern materialist wants us to believe, but also with a soul. He knew this in such a way that he could feel something like the following (although he could not have expressed it in these words, since the anthroposophy of today was not then available): The Christ-Impulse has been received by the soul of the Earth into its aura, and someone whose soul feels imbued with the Earth's aura, and with the Christ-Impulse, may again look up to what is written in the stars. And in fact this was done; people did look up to the stars. Although this approach brought with it a great deal of superstition, especially among the old astronomers who appeared at that time, yet we find a certain man, deeply bound up with the spiritual life of the new epoch, writing in this way:

> These and countless other changes and phenomena which take place on the Earth are so exact and regular that they cannot be ascribed to a blind cause, and since the planets themselves know nothing of the angles which their rays make with the Earth, the Earth must have a soul. The Earth is an animal. [He does not mean an animal in the ordinary sense, but a living organism.] One can observe in the Earth a complete analogy with the parts of an animal body. Plants are its hair; metals are its veins; the waters of the sea are its drink. The Earth has a formative power, a kind of imagination; it has movement, certain

illnesses, and ebb and flow are its respirations. The soul of the Earth seems to be a kind of flame; hence the subterranean warmth and the fact that without warmth there is no propagation. A certain image of the Zodiac and of the whole firmament is imprinted by God in the soul of the Earth.

This is the bond between the heavens and the Earth, the cause of sympathy between heaven and Earth; the archetypes of all these movements and functions are implanted by God the Creator in the Earth. The soul is in the centre of the Earth; it sends out forms or impressions of itself in all directions, and in this way experiences all harmonious changes and objects outside itself. As it is with the soul of the Earth, so is it with the soul of man. All mathematical ideas and proofs, for example, are created by the soul from out of itself, or they would not have such a high degree of certainty and precision.

The planets and their aspects have influence on the soul-powers of men. They stir up emotions and passions of all kinds, leading often to the most terrible actions and events. They have influence on conception, and therefore on human temperament and character; a great part of astrology has to do with this. Probably the Sun does not only radiate light and warmth throughout the cosmos; it may also be the seat and centre of pure reason and the source of universal harmony. And all the planets are ensouled.

In the whole creation there is a magnificent and wonderful harmony, in the realm of the senses as well as in the supra-sensible, in ideas as well as in things, in the kingdoms of nature and in the gifts of Grace. This harmony is found both in things themselves and in the relations between them. The highest harmony is God, and He has impressed on all souls an inner harmony as his signature. Numbers, shapes, the stars, and nature in general, harmonize with certain mysteries of the Christian religion. Thus for example in the cosmos there are three things at rest, the Sun, the fixed stars, and the intermedium, and all else is in movement; and so in the one God are Father, Son and Holy Spirit. The sphere represents the Trinity: the Father is the centre, the Son the surface, and the Holy Spirit the uniformity of the distance from centre to surface (the radius); and so it is with other mysteries. Without spirits and souls there would not be harmony everywhere. In human souls, we find harmonious pre-dispositions of an endlessly varied kind. The whole Earth is ensouled, and thus the great harmony is brought about, not only on Earth, but between the Earth and the constellations. This soul works throughout the body of the Earth,

> but it has its seat in a particular place, just as the human soul has its seat in the heart; and from this place, as though from a focus or source, its workings go out into the ocean and the atmosphere. Hence the sympathy between the Earth and the stars; hence the regularity of nature's processes. The fact that the Earth truly has a soul is shown most clearly by observing weather conditions and the aspects under which they habitually occur. Under certain aspects and constellations the air is always restless; if such aspects are not present, or are few or transient, the air remains quiet.

Thus wrote a man in 1607; a man in whom lived and pulsed, as the new age came in, the Christ-filled astrology which draws after it, merely as its shadow, astrological superstition. Thus wrote a man out of the most devout mood of soul; a man who knew that people had formerly made use—at first rightly and afterwards wrongly—of the forces that spring from the elemental world, the sibylline forces we should now call them. For it cannot be denied, he wrote, that such spirits—he means spirits which maintain communication between the stars and the Earth—establish themselves in the elements which surround the Earth as its atmosphere. He continues:

> It cannot be denied that such spirits formerly imparted their oracular sayings to men through idols and oak trees, out of groves and grottoes, through animals and so on; and sooth-saying from the flight of birds was not merely an art of deceiving the weak. Those spirits were active in guiding the birds through the air, and by this means, with God's permission, much was intimated to men in former times. Even today we hear stories of fateful birds, such as owls, vultures, eagles, ravens, but the more such stories are despised, the rarer they become. For these spirits cannot bear being despised, as according to the law of God and Christian teaching, they certainly deserve to be: they prefer to fly away and keep silent. From the beginning, the lying Tempter was allowed to speak through animals: he spoke to Eve through the serpent and thus he led the human race astray. That was always the way of these spirits from then onwards: whenever they could speak to men through the bodies and movements of animals, through voices or portents, they misused this power, appropriating for themselves the reverence due to God and misleading unhappy men. And now, although Christ came to destroy the work of the Devil, and imposed silence on these spirits, and although they lost their temple statues, their groves and their caves

> and the Earth they had so long possessed, yet they are always here still in the empty air, and with God's permission they utter their scattered cries. Often they are God's scourges; often he allows certain things to be announced through them to humans.

The author of these words gives a gentle indication of how the spiritual revelations come to be permeated by Christ, for he writes in a frame of mind that can truly be called Christ-filled. In 1607 he spoke thus of the changes that had come about in the spiritual world. Who is this man? Is he someone who has no right to speak, someone we can leave unheard? No, for without him we should have no modern astronomy or physics: he is *Johannes Kepler.*[55] And one would like to advise those who call themselves materialists or monists and look to Kepler as their idol—one would like to advise them to consider carefully, just for once, this passage in Kepler's writings. The greatest astronomical laws, the three laws of Kepler, which dominate present-day astronomy, are his. Yet you have heard how he speaks of the new influence that gradually enters into earthly evolution with the fifth post-Atlantean epoch. We must all again get accustomed by degrees—having thoroughly absorbed the new influence—to recognize something of the spiritual activities connected with the stars.

What sort of time was it, then, when Parsifal entered the Grail Castle, still ignorant, not ready to ask questions—according to the later tradition taken up by Wolfram von Eschenbach?[56] What sort of time was it when Parsifal entered the Castle, where Amfortas lay wounded and on Parsifal's arrival suffered unceasing pain from his wound? What was this time? The saga itself tells us—it was a Saturnine time. Saturn and the Sun stood together in Cancer, approaching culmination. So we see how in the most intimate effects a connection between the Earth and the Stars is established. It was a Saturnine time!

And if we now ask how Parsifal gradually gains knowledge, what do we find? Who is he, this Parsifal? He is ignorant of certain things; he is held to be ignorant—but of what? Now we have heard that the Christ-Impulse flows on as though through subterranean channels in the depths of the soul. Up above, the theological controversies go on, and from them traditional Christianity takes shape. Let us follow the personality of Parsifal, as the saga portrays him. He knows nothing about the surface course of events; he is kept in ignorance precisely of all that. He is protected from it. What he learns to know comes from sources active in the depths of the soul, as we heard yesterday. At first, riding away in ignorance from the Grail Castle, he learns it from the woman who mourns the dead bridegroom in her lap; then from the hermit, who is brought into connection with mystic powers; and from the power of the Grail, for it is on a Good Friday that he comes to the hermit; already the power of the Grail is working in him unconsciously. Thus he is one of those who know nothing of what has been going on externally; one of those who are led into relation with the influences flowing from unconscious sources to meet the new age. He is a one whose heart and soul were to receive in innocence, undisturbed by the effects of the external world on human life, the secret of the Grail. He is to receive the secret with the highest, purest, noblest forces of the soul. He has to meet someone who has not developed the inner forces that could completely experience the Grail: he has to meet Amfortas. We know that Amfortas had indeed been marked out as the Guardian of the Grail, but he succumbed to the lower forces in human nature. And how he had succumbed is connected with the guardianship of the Grail: he had killed his adversary out of lust and jealousy. These things are obvious, but as they are repeatedly misunderstood, it must be said that anthroposophy does not teach asceticism. Something much deeper lies behind.

As late as the third post-Atlantean epoch there were natural elemental forces which were taken into consideration not so much for the way in which they were expressed in daily life as for the connection they revealed with the spiritual world. The elemental forces that pulsed in the human blood and nervous system were raised into a relationship with the Mysteries. It was not a question of subjecting the senses to ascetic discipline, but of becoming aware of the Holy Mysteries. In the third post-Atlantean epoch, one could still come to the Mysteries with the same forces which otherwise dominate humans on Earth. But the time was at hand when the Holy Mysteries were to be revealed only to the pure and blameless forces of the soul; when humans would find the possibility of rising above the bonds which tie them to an earthly calling. Anthroposophy does not seek to estrange anyone from the Earth; but it was then a question of raising oneself above those earthly ties and from the influence of the old astrology. Humans had to raise themselves if they were to find the old Mysteries in the new way—with the powers of the innocent soul that had freed itself from everything earthly.

Over against the contrast set up by Hebrew antiquity, another contrast had to be created. Hebrew antiquity had rigorously insisted: 'Nothing of the Sibylline forces, which were justified at one time in astrology—nothing of them! Let us cleave to our earthly god, Yahweh!' From this came a denial of all revelations from above and an acceptance of revelations from below; a fear of all that reveals itself from the heavens. This outlook had to prevail on Earth for a season; a certain opposition to anything that came from above had to establish itself. And in such forces as those of the sibyls people saw the unlawful luciferic forces coming from above. But presently, after the Christ had descended into the body of Jesus of Nazareth, that which came from above was imbued with the Christ-Impulse; humans could venture again to look up to the heavens. And something else had come about through the union of the Ruler of Earth with the Moon-Mother. For the Christ, Who had poured Himself out into the Earth's aura, had become the Lord of the Earth.

Worldly concerns, such as were pursued at the court of King Arthur, could be approached with earthly forces, but it was not permitted to approach the concerns of the Holy Grail in this way, as Amfortas had found. Anyone who attempted it was bound to suffer pain. And since the working of the stars had been permeated by the Christ, a man had to be found who had remained untouched by the controversies in the external world, and through his karma stood at a point where his soul could be approached by Christ; a man, too, who was related to the forces indicated by the symbol of the Saturnine time, with Saturn and the Sun standing together in the sign of Cancer. So it was that Parsifal, in whom the Christ-Impulse was still working unconsciously, in the depths of his soul, comes with the power of Saturn; and the wound burns as it had never burnt before.

Thus we see how the new age declares itself; how the soul of Parsifal is related to the new, subconscious, historical impulse permeated by Christ's aura, the Christ-Impulse, although he knows nothing of it. But the forces which had guided human history from below the surface were gradually to emerge; and Parsifal, accordingly, had to come by degrees to understand something that will never be understood unless it is approached with the pure and blameless forces of the soul, and not with traditional knowledge and scholarship. Then we can see—for this has by now come to the surface and is almost as familiar as the name of the Holy Grail itself—how it represents the renewing in a different form of what ancient Hebraism had fought in its day.

Let us set before us the Virgin Mother with the Christ upon her knees and let us then express it thus: He who can feel the holiness of this picture will feel the same for the Holy Grail. Above all other lights, all other gods, shines the Holy Vessel—the Moon-Mother now touched by Christ, the new Eve, the bearer of the Spirit of the Sun, Christ.

Think of the 'what', but still more of the 'how'![57] And let us look into the soul of Parsifal: how, riding out from the Grail Castle, he encounters the sight of the bride and bridegroom, which brings him into connection with subconscious forces of Christ. Let us look how the hermit at Eastertide, when the picture of the Grail is written in the heavens, in the stellar script, gives instruction to Parsifal's pure soul. Let us follow him as he rides on—as I emphasized yesterday—by day and night, looking at nature by day and with the symbol of the Holy Grail often before him at night; how he rides on, having before him the gold-gleaming sickle of the Moon, with the Host, the Spirit of Christ, the Spirit of the Sun, within it. Let us see how on his way he is made ready to understand the secret of the Holy Grail by the concordance between the picture of the Virgin Mother with her bridegroom Son and the sign of the heavenly script.

Let us see how the permeation of the Earth's destiny with the Christ-Impulse works together in his soul with the stellar script which has to be made new; let us see how all that is permeated with Christ is related to the forces of the stars. ... Since Parsifal had to enter the Grail Castle at a Saturnine time, it was inevitable that the wounds of the man, Amfortas, who had failed to abide rightly by the Grail should burn more fiercely.

Think of the 'what', but still more of the 'how'! For it is not a question of characterizing such things with the words I have been using, or with any words. There is no way of approach to the Grail through words of any kind, or through philosophical speculations. The only way is by changing all these words into feeling, by becoming able to feel in the Grail the sum of all that is holy, by feeling the confluence of that which came over from the Ancient Moon, appearing first in the Earth-Mother, Eve, and then newly in the Virgin Mother; of the God Yahweh who became Ruler of the Earth, and of the coming of the Christ, Who poured Himself into the Earth's aura and became the new Lord of the Earth; by feeling the confluence of that which works down from the stars, and is symbolized in the stellar script, with human evolution on Earth. If one takes all this into account and feels it as the consonance of human history with the stellar script, then one also grasps the secret that was to be expressed in the words entrusted to Parsifal in the saga: that whenever a King of the Grail, a truly appointed Guardian of the Grail, dies, the name of his accredited successor appears on the Holy Grail. 'There it is to be read'—which means that it will be necessary to learn to read the stellar script again in a new form.

Let us try to make ourselves worthy to do this; let us try to read the stellar script in the form now given to us. For in fact it is nothing else than a reading of the script when we try to trace our human evolution through Ancient Saturn, Sun, and Moon, right up to the Vulcan period. But we must recognize in what connection we wish to decipher the stellar script today. Let us make ourselves worthy of it! For not in vain are we told that the Grail was at first carried away from its own place and for a season was not externally perceptible. Let us regard what we are permitted to study in our anthroposophy as a renewed seeking for the Grail, and let us try to learn to understand the significance of that which formerly spoke as though out of the subconscious depths of the soul and rose gradually into human consciousness. Let us try to transform that by degrees into a new and more conscious language! Let us try to explore a wisdom that will disclose to us the connection between the earthly and the heavenly, not relying on old traditions, but in accordance with the way in which it can be revealed today.

And then let us be filled with a feeling of how it was that Parsifal came to the secret of the Grail. Afterwards the secret was kept hidden again, because humans had first to seek for the connection of the Earth with cosmic powers in the most external field, the field of the most external science. Let us also understand how it was that a spirit such as Kepler's could in the meantime come to grasp what he set out in his mathematical and mechanical laws of the heavens; but what he added to this, being truly penetrated with the Christ-Impulse, had to sink back into the subconscious depths of the soul. When we express what we know how to say today about the evolution of our Earth and its connection with the cosmos, we are speaking in Kepler's sense. Thus we have heard him say:

> Thus for example in the cosmos there are three things at rest, the Sun, the fixed stars, and the inter-medium, and all else is in movement; and so in the one God are Father, Son and Holy Spirit. The sphere represents the Trinity: the Father is the centre, the Son the surface, and the Holy Spirit the uniformity of the distance from centre to surface (the radius); and so it is with other mysteries. Without spirits and souls there would not be harmony everywhere. In human souls we find harmonious pre-dispositions of an endlessly varied kind. The whole Earth is ensouled, and thus the great harmony is brought about, not only on Earth but between the Earth and the constellations. This soul works throughout the body of the Earth, but it has its seat in a particular place, just as the human soul has its seat in the heart; and from this place, as though from a focus or source, its workings go out into the ocean and the atmosphere. Hence the sympathy between the Earth and the stars; hence the regularity of nature's processes. The fact that the Earth truly has a soul is shown most clearly by observing weather conditions and the aspects under which they habitually occur. Under certain aspects and constellations the air is always restless; if such aspects are not present, or are few or transient, the air remains quiet.
>
> These and countless other changes and phenomena which take place on the Earth are so exact and regular that they cannot be

> ascribed to a blind cause, and since the planets themselves know nothing of the angles which their rays make with the Earth, the Earth must have a soul. The Earth is an animal. One can observe in the Earth a complete analogy with the parts of an animal body. Plants are its hair; metals are its veins; the waters of the sea are its drink. The Earth has a formative power, a kind of imagination; it has movement, certain illnesses, and ebb and flow are its respirations. The soul of the Earth seems to be a kind of flame; hence the subterranean warmth and the fact that without warmth there is no propagation. A certain image of the Zodiac and of the whole firmament is imprinted by God in the soul of the Earth.

We see today how this picture of the Zodiac has been imprinted on the soul of the Earth, the aura of the Earth, and let us work gradually towards the other part of Kepler's worldview—the part which had to remain in the subconscious depths of the soul, but shows clearly that what we can give today as a cosmology is a fulfilment of it. Just as our anthroposophy—or what anthroposophy should mean to us—must be deeply grounded in the evolution of humanity, so is it inwardly connected with the admonition which resounds to us from the Holy Grail. And if we look at Europe, the Western land of ancient times, and see what memories of the Atlantean epoch lived on into post-Atlantean times; if we see how in the Greek world a last faint echo sounded, showing how the Nathan Jesus had once been permeated by the Christ in the higher worlds, the Jesus who then descended and accomplished the Mystery of Golgotha—then, if we follow that out, we may ask: Whence did the Christ come? How did He come when He came from on high to be the Lord of the Earth? He passed from the West to the East, and from the East He returned to the West. His external physical covering came down from the realm of the higher Hierarchies. The Beings of those Hierarchies brought it down; it belonged to them. The saga of Parsifal reminds us of this in a beautiful way when it says: 'A host of Angels brought to Titurel the Holy Grail, the true Mystery of the Christ Jesus, of the connection between the Lord of the Earth and the Virgin Mother; and a host of Angels awaits it again in the realm of the higher Hierarchies.' Let us seek it there; and then we shall gradually come to understand what our anthroposophical worldview is seeking; we shall gradually press on further and further towards a feeling, a perception, of the celestial aspect of the Holy Grail and thence to its human aspect, to the Mother with Jesus, the Christ.

Thus we have tried to point the way a little into the realm of human history, in so far as human history is sustained by spiritual powers. And if you have perceived something of what I wished to arouse through my words, not only in your thoughts but in your feeling, the aim of this cycle of lectures will have been achieved. I could quite as well have called it 'Concerning the Search for the Holy Grail'. It can be left to each individual to judge whether the religious faiths scattered over the Earth will one day find themselves in agreement with what is here meant by the harmony of all religions. And he can decide also whether what should be understood by the unity of religions is not more closely related to the secret of the Holy Grail, as we have tried to describe it, than is a great deal of talking about the unity of religions, which may in fact be about something quite different

Anyone who wishes to hold fast to a narrow creed will certainly not be immediately convinced by what has been said. This is because he pays heed to the superficial course of events, and so to the external aspect of the real deeds of Christ, which are themselves of a spiritual nature. How a man was led by his karma to the spiritual deeds of Christ; how Parsifal was driven along this path, wherein is prefigured the unity of religions on Earth—that is what we have wished to bring before our souls. And we should keep in mind that continuation of the Parsifal saga which says that when the Grail became invisible in Europe, it was carried to the realm of Prester John,[58] who had his kingdom on the far side of the lands reached by the Crusaders. In the time of the Crusades the kingdom of Prester John, the successor of Parsifal, was still honoured, and from the way in which a search was made for it we must say: If all this were expressed in terms of strict earthly geography, it would show that the place of Prester John is not to be found on Earth.

Was that meant to be a hint, in the European saga that continued the Parsifal saga, that since then, without our being conscious of it, the Christ has been working in the hidden depths of the

East; that the religious controversies which take their course on the conscious level in the East could be assuaged by the out-flowings and revelations of the true Christ-Impulse, as was meant to happen, in accordance with the Parsifal revelation, in the West? Was the Sun-light of the Grail called upon to shine above all other gods on Earth, as is symbolically indicated by the fact that when the maiden carried in the gold-gleaming vessel, with the secret of the Grail within it, the radiance of the Grail outshone the other lights? Ought we to expect—quite contrary to current beliefs—that the power of Christ, still working unconsciously, will appear in a changed form and as *Ex oriente lux*,[59] in the old phrase, will meet with that which has appeared as light in the West? Should one light be able to unite with the other light? But for that it will be necessary for us to be prepared—we who are placed by karma in the geographical and cultural environment over which passed the path of Christ, when in higher realms He had permeated Jesus of Nazareth in order to journey to the East. Let us look up and feel that the Christ passed through our heights before He was revealed on Earth! Let us make ourselves capable of so understanding Him that we shall not misunderstand what He will perhaps be able to say to us one day, when the time has come for His impulses to flow through other earthly creeds!

APPENDICES

Appendix 1

THE ETHERIC AND THE ASTRAL BODIES

'Etheric body' is Steiner's early, theosophical term for the subtle body of supra-physical forces that sustains life. Later he would also refer to it variously as 'the life body', or the 'formative forces body', or (echoing Spinoza's distinction between *natura naturans* and *natura naturata*) the realm of 'living working' as opposed to the physical realm of 'finished work'.

The etheric body is known through Imaginaton, and first reveals itself to strengthened thinking as supra-sensible pictures. The etheric body consists of centrifugal forces, expresses itself in all aqueous processes, and flows in great currents through the cosmos. The etheric is a 'time body'; here time becomes space. It is a unity that is always there as a temporal totality, right up to the present moment.

The individual etheric body is precipitated out of a vast cosmic ether. It can be subdivided further into warmth ether, light ether, chemical or tone ether, and life ether. Theodor Schwenk's *Sensitive Chaos: The Creation of Flowing Forms in Water and Air* (London: Rudolf Steiner Press, 1996) is a scientifically compelling and aesthetically beautiful exploration of these forces.

'Astral body' is Steiner's early, theosophical term for the subtle body that corresponds generally to 'soul' or 'psyche'. Like Freud and Jung, he sees it as internally differentiated and gradually transformed by the activity of the higher faculty of the 'I' or 'ego'. The astral body reveals itself to Inspiration, and emerges in a sense from behind Imagination. The traditional concept of the Music of the Spheres is an experience of macrocosmic astrality. It consists of centripetal forces, and expresses itself in breathing and in the airy element generally. It also expresses itself as the human nervous system.

The astral body has remained behind in time, and casts its beams forward into the present incarnation; it remains in the spiritual world before conception and birth.

The *locus classicus* for both of these bodies among Steiner's introductory works is the uncharacteristically schematic and static description in his early book *Theosophy* (1904; many English editions are available, including now very inexpensive ebook editions). A much more dynamic (but also much more difficult) account is to be found in the middle four lectures of Rudolf Steiner, *A Psychology of Body, Soul, & Spirit* (New York: SteinerBooks, 1999), which includes a valuable Introduction by Robert Sardello. See also Lecture 5 (2 February, 1924) of the cycle GA 234; *Anthroposophy and the Inner Life*, trans. and Intro. Owen Barfield (Bristol: Rudolf Steiner Press, 1994).

Appendix 2

PLATONISM AND ARISTOTELIANISM

Plato (left) and Aristotle, from Raphael's School of Athens

Plato (428-347 BCE) was a Greek philosopher. He founded the first public school of philosophy in Athens, the Academy, and he introduced into the discipline both dialogue and dialectics. His importance is hard to overestimate: indeed, Alfred North Whitehead wrote of the European philosophical tradition that it was nothing but a succession of footnotes to Plato. He is exceptional in that his full oeuvre seems to have been transmitted down through the ages intact. His immediate teacher was Socrates, and Aristotle was his student.

Aristotle (384-322 BCE) was also a Greek philosopher, and one of the greatest philosophers who ever lived. 'A prodigious researcher and writer, Aristotle left a great body of work, perhaps numbering as many as two-hundred treatises, from which approximately thirty-one survive. His extant writings span a wide range of disciplines, from logic, metaphysics and philosophy of mind, through ethics, political theory, aesthetics and rhetoric, and into such primarily non-philosophical fields as empirical biology, where he excelled at detailed plant and animal observation and description.' [*Stanford Encyclopedia of Philosophy*] He was the teacher of Alexander the Great.

Platonism inspired a large number of Neo-Platonists, the greatest being Plotinus. Plotinus (c. 204-270 CE) 'was a Platonic philosopher born in Lycopolis, Egypt. Although the story of his life was written down by his student Porphyry, few biographical details are included because Plotinus rejected the physical world of appearances in favour of the realm of the mind and considered trivialites such as his birth date, family, ancestry and personal endeavors unworthy of mention. At the age of 28 he began a course of study with the Platonist Ammonius Saccas that deeply impacted his life. Already a student of philosophy, Plotinus devoted himself fully to the discipline, absorbing Plato's Dialogues and his teacher's commentary on them. Plotinus' concept of the Divine Mind and the purpose of mortal existence exerted tremendous influence on all three of the world's great monotheistic religions and, for this reason, many consider him the most significant philosopher of the Ancient world. He is the founder of the school of thought known as Neo-Platonism; a significant number of famous ancient writers, theologians, politicians, generals, and philosophers are now recognized as Neo-Platonists, although they would not have referred to themselves by that label. Plotinus' philosophy was recorded in the Enneads by Porphyry; he wrote nothing himself. He died in Rome at the age of 66.' [ancient.eu]

The School of Chartres revived a form of Platonism, and thus can be called Neo-Platonic. In the Renaissance, the Florentine philosopher Marsilio Ficino (1433-1499) translated Plato into Latin, and was himself heavily influenced by Plato as a philosopher, as was Giovanni Pico della Mirandola (1463–1494). Indeed, the pair headed a philosophical school that is referred to as Florentine Neo-Platonism.

The most important Aristotelians were the Scholastics, and especially Thomas Aquinas. Among modern philosophers, Leibniz (1646-1716) and Hegel (1770-1831) stand out for their strong, if heavily modified, Aristotelianism.

Appendix 3

CHARLES DARWIN

Charles Darwin (1809-1882) was the pre-eminent English naturalist whose theory of evolution by natural selection and 'struggle for existence' has come to dominate biology.

Darwin's grandfather Erasmus was also a famous naturalist, and the author of *Zoonomia; or the Laws of Organic Life* (1794-1796). At 16, Darwin was an enthusiastic shooter of game and little else. His father sent him off to study medicine at Edinburgh University, which slowly began to pique his scientific interests. It was there he also had his first encounters with materialism and atheism. However, he was put off by various aspects of medicine, so his father decided he would study to join the clergy at Cambridge. There he reverted to many of his earlier habits.

Inspired by Alexander von Humboldt's accounts of his South American journeys, Darwin eagerly took up the offer to sail around the world on the HMS *Beagle*. He travelled as a self-financed gentleman and amateur. Darwin began to formulate the theory of evolution privately in 1837-1839 after returning from his voyage, but he did not give it full public expression until the publication of *The Origin of Species* (1859).

With an annual allowance of £400 from his father, Darwin settled into the comfortable life of a geologist. He was secretary of the Geological Society by 1838, and his fame grew with the publication of the diary from his journey and other geological tracts. His reading of Malthus's *Essay on the Principle of Population* was a turning point in the development of evolutionary theory. 'Darwin realized that population explosions would lead to a struggle for resources and that the ensuing competition would weed out the unfit. It was an idea he now applied to nature (he had previously thought that animal populations remained stable in the wild). Darwin called his modified Malthusian mechanism 'natural selection'. Nature was equally uncharitable, went the argument: overpopulated, it experienced a fierce struggle, and from all manner of chance variations, good and bad, the best, 'the surviving one of ten thousand trials', won out, endured, and thus passed on its improved trait' (*Britannica*).

In 1839, Darwin married his cousin Emma Wedgwood. He shared his ideas privately on evolution, shocking her deeply. Darwin wrote down a sketch of his theory in 1842, and expanded it in 1844, but he did not intend to publish it. Meanwhile, he became enormously wealthy. Perhaps he lost the last of his belief in Christianity when his eldest daughter, Annie, died of typhoid, although he wrote in his draft of *The Origin of Species* that he was a theist, and he later became not an atheist but an agnostic.[60]

He began to write his masterpiece, and 'had finished a quarter of a million words by June 18, 1858. That day he received a letter from Alfred Russel Wallace, an English socialist and specimen collector working in the Malay Archipelago sketching a similar-looking theory. Darwin, fearing loss of priority, accepted Lyell's and Hooker's solution: they read joint extracts from Darwin's and Wallace's works at the Linnean Society on July 1, 1858. Darwin was away, sick, grieving for his tiny son who had died from scarlet fever, and thus he missed the first public presentation of the theory of natural selection' (*Britannica*). The rhetoric of that document read on 1 July is shockingly harsh: he begins by arguing 'all nature is at war, one organism with another', claims that 'it is the doctrine of Malthus applied in most cases with tenfold force', and goes so far as to say 'nature may be compared to a surface on which rest 10,000 sharp wedges touching each other and driven inwards by incessant blows' (Simpson 20-21). One even wonders whether it's Darwin's voice speaking here, or somebody else's.

He quickly wrote a more accessible version of his theory, *The Origin of Species*, and the rest is history. Except that history is far more complicated than biology textbooks and Darwinian apologists make out. In his magisterial study, *The Structure of Evolutionary Theory* (Cambridge, Mass.: Harvard University Press, 2002), the late and great evolutionary biologist Stephen J. Gould compares Darwin's original thesis with contemporary evolutionary theory to the Romanesque basilica that has been transformed utterly to become Milan Cathedral. His final verdict on Darwin runs: 'I do believe that the Darwinian framework, and not just the foundation, persists in the emerging structure of a more adequate evolutionary theory. But I also hold … that substantial changes, introduced during the last half of the 20th century, have built a structure so expanded beyond the original Darwinian core, and so enlarged by new principles of macroevolutionary explanation, that the full exposition, while remaining within the domain of Darwinian logic, must be construed as basically different from the canonical theory of natural selection, rather than simply extended' (p. 3).

Appendix 4

MICHELANGELO AND THE MEDICI TOMBS

By Margot Amrine

Michelangelo Buonarroti (1475-1564), the artist and the human being, has fascinated royalty, scholars, artists, and travellers for centuries. His stunning technique serves great expressive goals; his life as a multifaceted, but solitary genius continues to inspire and amaze. Biographers were hard at work before he died, and many others followed. Like most Renaissance artists, he worked as a painter, sculptor, and architect. One of the three 'Renaissance Triumvirate' (along with

Leonardo and Raphael), he is considered one of the three greatest Italian sculptors of *all* times, joining Donatello and Bernini. A short list of excellent books follows.

Let us focus briefly on four topics: Renaissance ideals, tomb sculptures, the Medici family, and the phenomenon of the 'non-finito'. A separate section that follows will address the Medici tombs specifically.

Renaissance ideals overlapped with some of the cherished ideals of the Middle Ages, but included a new emphasis on civic pride and responsibility, and they were informed by the ideals of antiquity. There was a renewed interest in the literature, philosophy, and art of Graeco-Roman culture. When antique sculptures were found and excavated, there was tremendous excitement. Sadly, these works had lost the bright pigmentation and adornment they originally possessed, but the ancient understanding of the beauty of the human being was admired and celebrated. Renaissance writers moved to extol the dignity of each individual, and the meaning of life balanced between 'active' and 'contemplative' states.

Tomb sculptures were richly resonant of these ideals. Tomb sculptures memorialized the individual's life and agency, even if the portraits were not true likenesses. Often, Neoplatonic themes informed the sculptor's (or patron's) choices as well.

The Medici family was closely linked to Michelangelo's destiny. They are impossible to sum up. They were humanists, poets, republicans, despots, plotters, civic-minded, power-hungry, and more. They were certainly patrons of the arts, and they left a glorious legacy: among a multitude of gifts, they donated the entire Uffizi Museum to the public in 1743. The Medici patronized Michelangelo from his early teens.

Michelangelo was reluctant to finish his work. About two thirds of his sculptures are unfinished. This was a very rare occurrence before Michelangelo. Hence, the term 'non-finito', specifically with regard to him. Did he want his works to be more expressive? Was the mental activity of sculpting more important than craftsmanship? Was the process, rather than the product, paramount? These are questions to ponder when considering the Medici tombs.

The Medici Tombs

Not far from Brunelleschi's soaring and incomparable dome, the iconic symbol of Florence, is the Medici church of San Lorenzo. The façade is unfinished to this day. It was to have held 24 sculptures by Michelangelo, but the contract was annulled. Michelangelo was instead asked to create tomb sculptures for Lorenzo ('the Magnificent'), Giuliano ('the Magnificent'), and two younger Medici dukes with the same names. All four lions rest in the 'New Sacristy of San Lorenzo', otherwise known as the Medici Chapel.

Although Michelangelo worked on many sketches, only the tombs of the two younger dukes were sculpted.[61] One hesitates to write 'completed', because of Michelangelo's characteristic 'non-finito' style. The statue of Lorenzo shows a thoughtful, contemplative individual, while that of Giuliano reflects an active life. However, the faces are not portraits, and some have suggested the titles are reversed. Below each is a pair of reclining figures resting on a curved sarcophagus lid, probably intended to suggest the arc of life, rising and falling, according to Dante.

Let us consider these four reclining figures. *Night* is the most famous. She seems to withdraw into herself, with symbols of death nearby: the owl, poppies, and an exceptional mask. At the same time he was sculpting *Night*, Michelangelo was painting *Leda and the Swan* (now lost, but which we know from a copy by Cornelis Bos). The poses are strikingly similar. Michelangelo wrote about *Night*: 'Do not wake me: pass with bated breath'. *Night* is highly polished, glistening. Opposite is *Day*, a male figure very much unfinished, twisting towards us. The other pair seem more subtle. *Dawn* is sensual, a Venus-type who seems as though she might rise. *Evening* is also a transitional figure, but male and less finished than *Dawn*.

What do these figures mean? Why these powerful nudes in the Sacristy, where communion is prepared? Do they represent the seasons, time and death, the four humours? In what way do they offer a picture of Neoplatonism? Does the Chapel relate to the Florentine cult of the Magi?

Not surprisingly, Rudolf Steiner's insights are original. He reads each of the four figures as a portrayal of one part of the fourfold human being. *Night* presents the etheric body; *Day* the ego; *Evening* the physical body; and *Dawn* the astral body. Steiner asserts that artists are inspired by the spiritual world. Looking at the statues, Steiner's scheme makes sense. *Day* is the least finished, just as our human ego is, and when we are confronted by his rough, yet piercing face, we wake up!

The Medici Chapel evokes wonder, questions, meditative thoughts. As we go to press in 2021, it has also become a very trendy topic. Why? The Chapel badly needed restoration, and an experimental technique succeeded. As reported in the *New York Times* (31 May, 2021),[62] a team of six Italian women (scientists, art restorers, art historians) used specific, nonhazardous strains of bacteria to eat the grime of centuries. The splendid Carrara marble, personally chosen by Michelangelo, has been renewed. The artist's genius shines forth. In one of his sonnets, Michelangelo wrote: 'The finest artist cannot conceive a thought that the marble itself does not bind within its shell, waiting to be brought out by the hand that serves the artist's mind.' The restorers left one small patch untouched (behind the sarcophagus of Giuliano) to show the contrast with the cleaned marble. A little nod to the non-finito perhaps.

Bibliography

- Beck, James. *Three Worlds of Michelangelo*. W. W. Norton, 1999.
- Gill, Anton. *Il Gigante*. St Martin's Press, 2002.
- Goffen, Rona. *Renaissance Rivals*. Yale, 2002.
- King, Ross. *Michelangelo and the Pope's Ceiling*. Walker, 2003.
- Pope-Hennessy, John. *Italian High Renaissance and Baroque Sculpture*. Phaidon, 1996.
- Scigliano, Eric. *Michelangelo's Mountain*. Free Press, 2005.

I am indebted to the late Ward Bissell, whose course on Renaissance sculpture at the University of Michigan was life changing. Thankfully, I took good notes, and kept them.

Appendix 5

COSMIC EVOLUTION

Steiner's account of cosmic evolution is grand beyond all imagining. Steiner affirmed the reality of evolution, but not as Darwin understood it. He honoured Darwin's theory, which was the inspiration and the precondition for Steiner's own research into what one might better term evolutionary cosmology. The same process Darwin describes from an earthly perspective as a gradually *ascending* evolution of increasingly complex biological forms, Steiner describes from a spiritual perspective as a gradual *descent* of spiritual entities into ever more adequate material vessels. In other places, Steiner offers additional perspectives on his cosmology, complementing the 'outer' view of the finished products in *Esoteric Science*, for example, with an especially sublime cycle of five short lectures offering, as it were, an 'Elohim's-eye view' of the same unfolding process.

In Steiner's account, humanity was created from the top down, but it has evolved from the bottom up, over successive 'incarnations' of Earth evolution proper, which was preceded by Saturn, Sun, and Moon. Evolution allows us to approach multiple goals: over many eons, we have been guided from simplicity toward complexity, from unconsciousness toward consciousness, from passivity toward activity, and from necessity toward freedom. Having received the gift of wisdom, our task is now to internalize that wisdom and transform it into active love. The paradox of freedom implies that the further we progress towards these goals, the less certain is the outcome of the process, which will increasingly be placed into our own hands.

The central texts are:

- Chapter 4 of CW 13, *An Outline of Esoteric Science* (Great Barrington. Massachusetts: SteinerBooks, 1997);

- CW 132, *Inner Experiences of Evolution* (Great Barrington, Massachusetts: SteinerBooks, 2009);
- CW 136, *Spiritual Beings in the Heavenly Bodies and in the Kingdoms of Nature* (Great Barrington, Massachusetts: SteinerBooks, 2012);
- CW 110, *The Spiritual Hierarchies and the Physical World: Zodiac, Planets and Cosmos*, trans. René M. Querido (Great Barrington, NY: SteinerBooks, 2008);
- and GA 122, *Genesis: Secrets of Creation* (2002; London: Rudolf Steiner Press, 2012).

Appendix 6

THE HIERARCHIES

Steiner's complex and highly esoteric ontology affirms the longstanding spiritual teaching that humans occupy a developmental stage between animals 'beneath' and angelic beings 'above' us. ('Beneath' and 'above' are meant to indicate relatively lower and higher levels of consciousness, developmental complexity, and power.) Arthur O. Lovejoy's eponymous study of 1936, which is widely viewed as the founding document of modern intellectual history, called this idea 'The Great Chain of Being', and that is now the conventional term for this set of ideas. This idea is in keeping with a Christian tradition extending back through Thomas Aquinas to Dionysius the Areopagite (late fifth or early sixth century CE; now referred to as 'Pseudo-Dionysius' to distinguish him from his much-earlier namesake), and ultimately to St Paul. In his treatise *On the Celestial Hierarchy* (Pseudo-Dionysius, *The Complete Works* [Mahwah, NJ: Paulist Press, 1987], pp. 143-192), Pseudo-Dionysius had distinguished nine ranks of beings 'above' humans in the spiritual or intelligible world: in ascending order, he terms them 'Angels', 'Archangels', and 'Principalities' (together the 'Third Hierarchy'); 'Authorities', 'Powers', and 'Dominions' (among other current translations; together the 'Second Hierarchy'); and 'Thrones', 'Cherubim', and 'Seraphim' (together the First Hierarchy). Steiner tends to refer to the Third and Second Hierarchies by their Greek names: 'Angeloi', 'Archangeloi', 'Archai'; 'Exousiai', 'Dynameis', and 'Kyriotetes.' Another set of terms Steiner often employs is 'Spirits of Form' (rather than 'Exousiai'), 'Spirits of Movement' (rather than 'Dynameis'), 'Spirits of Wisdom' (rather than 'Kyriotetes'), and 'Spirits of Will' (rather than Thrones). Among Steiner's many discussions of the hierarchies, the most fundamental are Ch. 4 of CW 13: *An Outline of Esoteric Science*, trans. Catherine E. Creeger (Great Barrington, MA: SteinerBooks, 1997); CW 136: *Spiritual Beings in the Heavenly Bodies and in the Kingdoms of Nature* (Great Barrington, MA: SteinerBooks, 2012); and CW 110: *The Spiritual Hierarchies and the Physical World: Zodiac, Planets and Cosmos*, trans. René M. Querido (Great Barrington, NY: SteinerBooks, 2008).

Appendix 7

AHRIMAN AND LUCIFER

Rudolf Steiner spoke often about the dual nature of evil, ascribing its source to supersensible beings he calls Lucifer and Ahriman. Lucifer might be termed the 'red devil,' who tempts humans to sin on the side of *superbia*: pride, anger, egotism, erotic passions, etc. 'Ahriman' is a traditional name for a black demon, beginning with the Zoroastrian figure Angra Mainyu, opponent of the Sun God Ahura Mazda. Ahriman's temptations are those of *acedia*: laziness, greed, and denial of the spirit generally.

Lucifer incarnated in the third millennium BCE, in the distant East. Ahriman will incarnate in the twenty-first century, in the West. Lucifer wants us to live in the past, while Ahriman cuts us off from the past. Lucifer wants us to flee the Earth; Ahriman wants to bind us to the Earth. Lucifer is responsible for the glories of pagan culture, which, however, provided no moral impulses. He longs for his cosmic home, which is the planet Venus. Ahriman seeks to subvert culture by promoting materialism, utility, nationalism, and literalism. He wants to reduce the freedom of the spiritual-cultural sphere to politics and economics. He wants to reduce all qualities to quantities.

Steiner argues that the assaults of these beings are providential: only by overcoming their resistance and holding them in proper balance can humanity become inwardly strong enough to develop genuine freedom, knowledge and love. Both figures are represented in Steiner's monumental sculpture *The Group* (from which these photos have been taken). In *The Group*, Christ as the Representative of Humanity shows us how to hold the balance: he does not vanquish Lucifer and Ahriman, but he keeps each in their place, restricting their activity.

For an excellent discussion of Steiner's ideas as applied to Goethe's *Faust*, see Alan P. Cottrell, *Goethe's View of Evil and the Search for a New Image of Man in our Time* (Edinburgh: Floris Press, 1982). Mephistopheles in Goethe's *Faust* exhibits traits of both beings by turns, and Steiner was critical of Goethe for having conflated them. Lucifer and Ahriman also appear as characters in Steiner's own expressionist *Mystery Dramas* (1910-1913): see GA 14, Rudolf Steiner, *Four Mystery Dramas*, trans. Ruth and Hans Pusch (Great Barrington, MA: SteinerBooks, 2007).

Ahriman

Lucifer (both taken from Rudolf Steiner's sculpture of 'The Representative of the Human Being')

Appendix 8

JOHANN WOLFGANG VON GOETHE

Goethe, age 38, painted by Angelica Kauffman (1787)

Johann Wolfgang von Goethe (1749-1832), author of the drama *Faust* and the novel *Wilhelm Meister* among many other works, is widely regarded as the greatest German poet. His lyrics, especially the late collection entitled *The West-Eastern Divan*, in imitation of the medieval Persian poet Hafiz, are unexampled in German. The first of the two *Wilhelm Meister*-novels, *Wilhelm Meister's Apprenticeship*, is surely the most influential novel in all of German literary history. And the two parts of *Faust* are viewed as a great pinnacle of German culture.

He was also an extraordinary scientist: see his *Metamorphosis of Plants* (1790) and his *Theory of Color* (1810) especially. The standard English translation of Goethe's scientific works is Johann Wolfgang von Goethe, *Scientific Studies*, vol. 12 of the Suhrkamp Edition [in English], ed. and trans. Douglas Miller (New York: Suhrkamp Publishers, 1988). A more recent edition of Miller's translation of *The Metamorphosis of Plants* (Cambridge, MA: MIT Press, 2009) includes glorious colour photographs of the plants Goethe discusses and a fine Introduction by the Director of the Environmental Studies Program at Seattle University, Gordon L. Miller.

As a young man, Steiner edited Goethe's scientific writings twice, including the definitive critical edition known as the *Weimarer* or *Sophien-Ausgabe*. The most important of Steiner's writings on Goethe's scientific work are contained in GA 1, GA 2, and GA 6. The latest English edition of GA 1 is a handsome offering from the Anthroposophic Press, *Nature's Open Secret: Rudolf Steiner's Introductions to Goethe's Scientific Works* (2000); earlier translations can still be found: *Goethe the Scientist* (New York: Anthroposophic Press, 1950), and *Goethean Science* (Spring Valley, NY: Mercury Press, 1988). See also CW 2; *Goethe's Theory of Knowledge: An Outline of the Epistemology of His Worldview* (Great Barrington, MA: SteinerBooks, 2008), and GA 6; *Goethe's Worldview* (Spring Valley, NY: Mercury Press, 1985).

The secondary literature on Goethe's science is vast. For a comprehensive bibliography through to 1990, see Frederick Amrine, *Goethe in the History of Science*, 2 vols. (New York: Peter Lang, 1996), which was compiled as an attempt to demonstrate in the greatest possible detail the extraordinary range and persistence of Goethe's influence. Frederick Amrine, Francis J. Zucker and Harvey Wheeler, eds., *Goethe and the Sciences: A Reappraisal*, Boston Studies in the Philosophy of Science 97 (Dordrecht: D. Reidel, 1987), contains many outstanding essays, and also a more concise bibliography.

APPENDIX 9

GANGANDA GREIDA

THE expression occurs in an old legend of Parsifal written in the Nordic language (akin to modern Icelandic). The legend originated in the thirteenth century and was probably based on Chrétien de Troyes. The Grail is here called 'ganganda greida'—from *gehend*, moving or going about, and *greida*, meaning literally 'things' and in this context indicating 'provisions' or 'nourishment'.

The legend is from a collection entitled *Riddararsögur* (*Rittersagen* = Legends of Knighthood), ed. by Eugen Kölbing, Strassburg, 1872.

For readers of German a most valuable book on the tremendous subject of the Grail is *Der Gral und seine Hüter* (The Grail and its Guardians) by Rudolf Meyer (Stuttgart: Verlag Urachhaus, 1956). See pages 25 and 289.

The following passages from Lectures 6 and 7 of the lecture-course given by Steiner at The Hague, March 1913 (*The Effect of Occult Development upon the Self and the Sheaths of Man*) help to convey the aspect of the Grail specifically conveyed in the expression 'ganganda greida'—i.e. *Wegzehrung*, nourishment or food while journeying along a path:

> The legend of the Holy Grail tells us of that miraculous food which is prepared from the finest activities of the sense-impressions and the finest activities of the mineral, extracts, whose purpose it is to nourish the noblest part of man all through the life he spends on Earth; for it would be killed by anything else. This heavenly food is what is contained in the Holy Grail ... [from Lecture 6].
>
> ... We have heard what the Holy Grail contains. It contains that by which the physical instrument of man on Earth must be nourished: the extract, the pure mineral extract which is obtained from all foods

and which unites in the purest part of the human brain with the purest sense-impressions, impressions which come to us through our senses. Now, to whom is this food to be handed? It is really to be handed—as is revealed to us when from the exoteric story we enter into the esoteric presentation of it in the Mysteries—it is really to be handed to the human being who has obtained the understanding of what makes man mature enough gradually to raise himself consciously to what the Holy Grail is ... [from Lecture 7].

Notes

Sources: The lectures were recorded in shorthand and transcribed into plain text by the stenographers. Shorthand transcripts were thought to be lost (the first German edition was printed more or less unchanged in later editions). In the meantime it has been ascertained that the original shorthand reports by Mrs Reebstein-Lehm and Clara Michels are still available. As a result of the latter, some difficult-to-understand passages in the present edition have been improved. It is unclear from which shorthand the printing was made at the time. During the review, some other errors that distorted the meaning were corrected. Some stylistic changes were also made.

The title of the volume: Rudolf Steiner gave the course under the title 'Christ and the Spiritual World'. The subtitle appeared after the first edition of the book in 1934, added by Marie Steiner.

Works by Rudolf Steiner within the *Gesautausgabe* (GA) are given in the references with the bibliography number. See also the overview at the end of this volume.

1 'Impulse' is one of Steiner's favourite words. It crops up everywhere, and it is always (but only mildly) metaphorical. Because the term is so resolutely mechanistic, but its referent is invariably spiritual or cultural, the effect can be jarring. As is so easily done in German, Steiner will frequently coin new terms by conjoining them with other words, e.g. 'Faust-impulse', 'Resurrection-impulse', and 'I-impulse'. 'Christ-impulse' occurs very frequently, and it makes sense in the context of Steiner's view of Christianity as a cosmic event unfolding over eons, of which even the Incarnation is but a single chapter.

2 'The Mystery of Golgotha' is Steiner's favoured term for all that is more conventionally referred to as the Incarnation, the Passion, and the Resurrection. One of Steiner's earliest publications, his book *Christianity as Mystical Fact*, situates Christianity squarely within the context of ancient mystery religions (rather than mysticism, which the title might seem to imply). This important text is now volume 8 of Steiner's *Complete Works* in English, and the latest edition (New York: Anthroposophic Press, 1997) was both translated and introduced by a scholar and anthroposophist of great stature, Andrew Welburn. In the same spirit, Steiner also refers to 'the Easter Mystery'.

3 'The Mysteries' is the Greek term for schools and rites that were esoteric in the strong sense: neophytes were forbidden to divulge their teachings—in some cases (such as the Pythagoreans) on pain of death. The most important Mystery centres were in Eleusis, Samothrace, and Ephesus.

4 Stoicism was a Hellenistic philosophy founded by Zeno of Citium. It is one of the noblest schools of thought, placing a high premium on intellectual and moral perfection. The chief doctrines of high Stoicism were that the sage is above misfortune, and that virtue alone is sufficient to guarantee happiness. The most famous Stoics were Seneca and Marcus Aurelius.

5 Socrates (470-399 BCE), although he wrote nothing, had an enormous influence on the subsequent history of philosophy. A consummate rationalist, he was the teacher of Plato—indeed, many of Plato's Dialogues feature Socrates in a starring role. Despite his vast influence, he was in many ways an enigmatic and controversial figure.

6 See Appendix 1.

7 'From the perspective of anthroposophy Rudolf Steiner asserts that the Lower Devachan (or the Heavenly World) and Higher Devachan (or the World of Reason) are two "supersensible" realms, above the astral realm, associated with emotions and will impulse, respectively. In comparison, the mental realm is associated with thought.' [*Wikipedia*]

8 See Appendix 2.

9 *Der deutsche Monistenbund* was a scientific society founded in Jena in 1906 under the leadership of the eminent biologist Ernst Haeckel. It was a complex organization with competing factions, but its general tenor was materialist and anti-religious.

[10] An important cosmogonic theory known as the 'nebular hypothesis', and the ancestor of our contemporary 'solar nebular disk model'. It hypothesizes that the solar system was formed when a primordial nebula began to spin and formed planets through the resultant centrifugal force, and many found the explanation compelling because it seemed to explain the planets' circular and roughly coplanar orbits moving in the same direction as the Sun's rotation. It was first expounded fully by Immanuel Kant in his *Universal Natural History and Theory of the Heavens* [1755; multiple English editions available]. Pierre-Simon, Marquis de Laplace (1749-1827), the great French mathematician and astronomer who extended the Newtonian paradigm in his five-volume *Celestial Mechanics* (1799-1825) and other writings, developed the same theory independently and published it in his *System of the World* [1796; many English translations available]. Steiner often derides this hypothesis, so often demonstrated in school classrooms, for failing to account for the teacher-demiurge who sets the nebula in motion in the first place. (See e.g. the end of the lecture of January 18, 1921 in CW 323; *Interdisciplinary Astronomy*.)

[11] See Appendix 3.

[12] *Maya* is a theosophical term that Steiner uses frequently. It is a contraction of the Sanskrit terms *maha* [great], *a* [not or non-, like 'alpha privative' in Ancient Greek; cf. 'apolitical'], and *ya* [being]; hence, 'maya' means literally 'the great non-being'. It is illusory because it seems to exist, but ultimately does not.

[13] See above all Plato's *Timaios*.

[14] See Steiner's full account in GA 114; *According to Luke: The Gospel of Compassion and Love Revealed* (Great Barrington, Massachusetts: SteinerBooks, 2001).

[15] This is Steiner's term for the traditional poets and patriarchs of the Vedic religion. Steiner refers to them frequently as the founders of the Ancient Indian cultural epoch, and he asserts that they were real, historical personages rather than mythic figures.

[16] 'Egypto-Chaldean' is Steiner's theosophical term for a long epoch he sees as having ended ca. 747 BCE. He also calls it the third post-Atlantean epoch or age. The implication of the term is that the Egyptian, Sumerian and Babylonian cultures were in the vanguard of human cultural evolution during that period—quite a conventional notion after

all, despite the idiosyncrasy of the label. Because it has become a standard anthroposophical term, 'Chaldean' stands here rather that Sumerian and/or Babylonian, which would be more conventional in English.

17 Steiner's theosophical term for Antiquity; he sees it as having lasted from 747 BCE to 1413 CE. He also terms it the Graeco-Roman age or the Graeco-Latin period. The name implies that Greece and Rome were the 'vanguard' cultures during the period, i.e. the loci of innovation and progress. He sees other cultures such as Ancient India, Persia, and Egypt as having been the leaders during even earlier periods. Steiner's terminology is idiosyncratic here, but the underlying thoughts are commonplaces of intellectual history.

18 The Pythia was the priestess who held court at the Oracle of Delphi, a sanctuary dedicated to the Greek god Apollo. The Greeks believed that she channelled prophecies from Apollo himself, while steeped in a dreamlike trance.

19 Thales of Miletus (ca. 624-ca. 546 BCE) was an important pre-Socratic philosopher. Aristotle considered Thales to have been the first Greek philosopher, and Bertrand Russell credits him with having founded the whole of Western philosophy. An excellent resource on the pre-Socratics in English is G. S. Kirk and J. E. Raven, *The Presocratic Philosophers: A Critical History with a Selection of Texts* (Cambridge: Cambridge University Press, 1971).

20 See Appendix 2.

21 Publius Vergilius Maro (70 BCE-29 BCE), usually called Virgil or Vergil in English, was an Augustan Roman poet. He composed three classics of Latin literature: the *Eclogues*, the *Georgics*, and the *Aeneid*, an epic poem.

22 'The *Sibylline Books* (Latin: *Libri Sibyllini*) were a collection of oracular utterances, set out in Greek hexameters, that, according to tradition, were purchased from a sibyl by the last king of Rome, Tarquinius Superbus, and were consulted at momentous crises through the history of the Republic and the Empire. Only fragments have survived, the rest being lost or deliberately destroyed.' [*Wikipedia*]

23 Thomas of Celano (1185-1265 CE) was an Italian poet of the Franciscan Order. His hymn became the Requiem Mass; the lines quoted are from the beginning. They translate: 'The day of wrath, that day, / will dissolve the world in ashes: / (this is) the testimony of David along with the Sibyl.'

[24] 'The Fifth Post-Atlantean Cultural Epoch' is Rudolf Steiner's theosophical term for the current historical epoch, which began ca. 1413—i.e., with the Renaissance. Steiner correlated these historical epochs with the precession of the equinox through the signs of the zodiac, with each epoch lasting 2,160 years. He sees the Fifth as lasting until approximately 3573 CE.

[25] *Fable convenue* is French for 'a fable agreed upon'.

[26] See Appendix 4.

[27] The Apostolic Fathers are the earliest patriarchs and theologians of the Catholic Church.

[28] GA 17; *A Way of Self-Knowledge* and *The Threshold of the Spiritual World* (Great Barrington, Massachusetts: SteinerBooks, 2006).

[29] See Appendix 5.

[30] Translated as CW 13; *An Outline of Esoteric Science*, trans. Catherine E. Creeger (Great Barrington, MA: SteinerBooks, 1997). An otherwise excellent earlier translation by George Adams bore the unfortunate title *Occult Science.* At the time of writing, Steiner was the head of the Theosophical Society in Germany, and the word *Geheimwissenschaft* in his title was meant to echo Blavatsky's tome, *The Secret Doctrine.* Thus *The Secret Science* would be a far more accurate translation. CW 13 is now considered one of the four 'basic books' of anthroposophy.

[31] See Rudolf Steiner's lecture of 7 March, 1914.

[32] See Appendix 6.

[33] See Appendix 7.

[34] 'Yehoshua' is a Hebrew name meaning 'Jehovah is salvation'.

[35] Ahura Mazda is the god of the Sun in Zoroastrianism.

[36] In Zorastrianism, a kind of father-god, who gave birth to both Ahura Mazda and Ahriman.

[37] See Rudolf Steiner, *GA 122; Genesis: Secrets of Creation* (London: Rudolf Steiner Press, 2002). Rpt. 2012.

[38] See Appendix 8.

[39] The Italian Dominican philosopher, scientist, and theologian Giordano Bruno (1548-1600) was burned at the stake by the Catholic Church on February 17, 1600. See the classic study by Frances Yates, *Giordano Bruno and the Hermetic Tradition* (Chicago: University of Chicago Press, 1964).

[40] Numbers 13:16.

41 Hammurabi (c. 1728-1686 BCE), a King of Babylon, who is supposed to have established the oldest code of laws in the world.

42 Attis was a Greek vegetation god; in his self-mutilation, death, and resurrection he represents the fruits of the earth, which die in winter only to rise again in the spring.

43 Adonis is widely seen as a prime example of the archetypal dying-and-rising god.

44 Rudolf Steiner often indicates that Elijah, John the Baptist, the painter Raphael, and the poet and philosopher Novalis were all reincarnations of the same individual.

45 The Council of Nicea took place in 325 CE.

46 Constantine I, also known as Constantine the Great (c. 280-337), was the first Roman Emperor to embrace Christianity. He ascribed his many successes to divine intervention. He was poorly educated, and temperamentally impatient, but his faith was sincere.

47 'Croesus, (died *c.* 546 BC), last king of Lydia (reigned *c.* 560–546), who was renowned for his great wealth. He conquered the Greeks of mainland Ionia (on the west coast of Anatolia) and was in turn subjugated by the Persians.' [*Britannica*]

48 See Appendix 9.

49 The Akashic Record is a symbolic, spiritual script in which everything is recorded that has ever happened on Earth. It can be read by an initiate, and this is how the spiritual researcher can speak of things about which no historical records survive. Ervin László in *Science and the Akashic Field: An Integral Theory of Everything* (2004), based on ideas by Rudolf Steiner, posits 'a field of information' as the substance of the cosmos, which he calls 'Akashic field' or 'A-field'.

50 Chrétien de Troyes (c. 1130-1190 CE), a French writer, was the father of Arthurian Romance. He wrote five epics in all, including *Perceval.*

51 Translation by M. Cotterell.

52 Richard Wagner (1813-1883) was a German composer and theorist who is especially well known for his operas or 'music dramas', as he called them. He is considered a late Romantic. Among his most important works are the four-opera cycle *The Ring of the Nibelungs*, *Tristan and Isolde*, and *Parsifal.*

53 GA 126; *Occult History: Historical Personalities and Events in the Light of Spiritual Science* (Rudolf Steiner Press, 1982).

[54] Anatole France (1844-1924) was a French writer; the work cited here is his *Life of St Joan.*

[55] Kant pronounced the German mathematician and astronomer Johannes Kepler (1571-1630) the most rigorous thinker who ever lived. He is most famous for discovering and mathematically modelling the elliptical motions of the planets, and for major contributions toward the theory of gravitation eventually formalized by Newton.

[56] Wolfram von Eschenbach (c. 1170-c. 1220 CE) was a 'German poet whose epic *Parzival*, distinguished alike by its moral elevation and its imaginative power, is one of the most profound literary works of the Middle Ages.' [*Britannica*]

[57] This is a famous quote from Goethe's *Faust*, line 6992.

[58] Prester John was a legendary figure who was thought to have travelled to the Orient and successfully spread Christianity there.

[59] Latin for 'light comes from the East'.

[60] George Gaylord Simpson, *The Book of Darwin* (New York: Washington Square Press, 1982), p. 17.

[61] The Chapel also holds Michelangelo's startling, mysterious, expressive *Madonna and Child*, which will not be discussed here.

[62] The article is fascinating, but if you do happen upon it, please keep an open mind regarding Alessandro.

Rudolf Steiner's Collected Works

The German Edition of Rudolf Steiner's Collected Works (the *Gesamtausgabe* [GA] published by Rudolf Steiner Verlag, Dornach, Switzerland) presently runs to 354 titles, organized either by type of work (written or spoken), chronology, audience (public or other), or subject (education, art, etc.). For ease of comparison, the Collected Works in English [CW] follows the German organization exactly. A complete listing of the CWs follows with literal translations of the German titles. Other than in the case of the books published in his lifetime, titles were rarely given by Rudolf Steiner himself, and were often provided by the editors of the German editions. The titles in English are not necessarily the same as the German; and, indeed, over the past 75 years have frequently been different, with the same book sometimes appearing under different titles.

For ease of identification and to avoid confusion, we suggest that readers looking for a title should do so by CW number. Because the work of creating the Collected Works of Rudolf Steiner is an ongoing process, with new titles being published every year, we have not indicated in this listing which books are presently available. To find out what titles in the Collected Works are currently in print, please check our website at www.rudolfsteinerpress.com (or www.steinerbooks.org for US readers).

Written Work

CW 1 Goethe: Natural-Scientific Writings, Introduction, with Footnotes and Explanations in the text by Rudolf Steiner
CW 2 Outlines of an Epistemology of the Goethean World View, with Special Consideration of Schiller
CW 3 Truth and Science
CW 4 The Philosophy of Freedom
CW 4a Documents to 'The Philosophy of Freedom'
CW 5 Friedrich Nietzsche, A Fighter against His Time

CW 6	Goethe's Worldview
CW 6a	Now in CW 30
CW 7	Mysticism at the Dawn of Modern Spiritual Life and Its Relationship with Modern Worldviews
CW 8	Christianity as Mystical Fact and the Mysteries of Antiquity
CW 9	Theosophy: An Introduction into Supersensible World Knowledge and Human Purpose
CW 10	How Does One Attain Knowledge of Higher Worlds?
CW 11	From the Akasha-Chronicle
CW 12	Levels of Higher Knowledge
CW 13	Occult Science in Outline
CW 14	Four Mystery Dramas
CW 15	The Spiritual Guidance of the Individual and Humanity
CW 16	A Way to Human Self-Knowledge: Eight Meditations
CW 17	The Threshold of the Spiritual World. Aphoristic Comments
CW 18	The Riddles of Philosophy in Their History, Presented as an Outline
CW 19	Contained in CW 24
CW 20	The Riddles of the Human Being: Articulated and Unarticulated in the Thinking, Views and Opinions of a Series of German and Austrian Personalities
CW 21	The Riddles of the Soul
CW 22	Goethe's Spiritual Nature and its Revelation in 'Faust' and through the 'Fairy Tale of the Snake and the Lily'
CW 23	The Central Points of the Social Question in the Necessities of Life in the Present and the Future
CW 24	Essays Concerning the Threefold Division of the Social Organism and the Period 1915-1921
CW 25	Cosmology, Religion and Philosophy
CW 26	Anthroposophical Leading Thoughts
CW 27	Fundamentals for Expansion of the Art of Healing according to Spiritual-Scientific Insights
CW28	The Course of My Life
CW 29	Collected Essays on Dramaturgy, 1889-1900
CW 30	Methodical Foundations of Anthroposophy: Collected Essays on Philosophy, Natural Science, Aesthetics and Psychology, 1884-1901
CW 31	Collected Essays on Culture and Current Events, 1887-1901
CW 32	Collected Essays on Literature, 1884-1902
CW 33	Biographies and Biographical Sketches, 1894-1905
CW 34	Lucifer-Gnosis: Foundational Essays on Anthroposophy and Reports from the Periodicals 'Lucifer' and 'Lucifer-Gnosis,' 1903-1908
CW 35	Philosophy and Anthroposophy: Collected Essays, 1904-1923
CW 36	The Goetheanum-Idea in the Middle of the Cultural Crisis of the Present: Collected Essays from the Periodical 'Das Goetheanum,' 1921-1925

CW 37 Now in CWs 260a and 251
CW 38 Letters, Vol. 1: 1881-1890
CW 39 Letters, Vol. 2: 1890-1925
CW 40 Truth-Wrought Words
CW 40a Sayings, Poems and Mantras; Supplementary Volume
CW 42 Now in CWs 264-266
CW 43 Stage Adaptations
CW 44 On the Four Mystery Dramas. Sketches, Fragments and Paralipomena on the Four Mystery Dramas
CW 45 Anthroposophy: A Fragment from the Year 1910

Public Lectures

CW 51 On Philosophy, History and Literature
CW 52 Spiritual Teachings Concerning the Soul and Observation of the World
CW 53 The Origin and Goal of the Human Being
CW 54 The Riddles of the World and Anthroposophy
CW 55 Knowledge of the Supersensible in Our Times and Its Meaning for Life Today
CW 56 Knowledge of the Soul and of the Spirit
CW 57 Where and How Does One Find the Spirit?
CW 58 The Metamorphoses of the Soul Life. Paths of Soul Experiences: Part One
CW 59 The Metamorphoses of the Soul Life. Paths of Soul Experiences: Part Two
CW 60 The Answers of Spiritual Science to the Biggest Questions of Existence
CW 61 Human History in the Light of Spiritual Research
CW 62 Results of Spiritual Research
CW 63 Spiritual Science as a Treasure for Life
CW 64 Out of Destiny-Burdened Times
CW 65 Out of Central European Spiritual Life
CW 66 Spirit and Matter, Life and Death
CW 67 The Eternal in the Human Soul. Immortality and Freedom
CW 68 Public lectures in various cities, 1906-1918
CW 69 Public lectures in various cities, 1906-1918
CW 70 Public lectures in various cities, 1906-1918
CW 71 Public lectures in various cities, 1906-1918
CW 72 Freedom—Immortality—Social Life
CW 73 The Supplementing of the Modern Sciences through Anthroposophy
CW 73a Specialized Fields of Knowledge and Anthroposophy
CW 74 The Philosophy of Thomas Aquinas
CW 75 Public lectures in various cities, 1906-1918
CW 76 The Fructifying Effect of Anthroposophy on Specialized Fields
CW 77a The Task of Anthroposophy in Relation to Science and Life: The Darmstadt College Course
CW 77b Art and Anthroposophy. The Goetheanum-Impulse

CW 78 Anthroposophy, Its Roots of Knowledge and Fruits for Life
CW 79 The Reality of the Higher Worlds
CW 80 Public lectures in various cities, 1922
CW 81 Renewal-Impulses for Culture and Science—Berlin College Course
CW 82 So that the Human Being Can Become a Complete Human Being
CW 83 Western and Eastern World-Contrast. Paths to Understanding It through Anthroposophy
CW 84 What Did the Goetheanum Intend and What Should Anthroposophy Do?

Lectures to the Members of the Anthroposophical Society

CW 88 Concerning the Astral World and Devachan
CW 89 Consciousness—Life—Form. Fundamental Principles of a Spiritual-Scientific Cosmology
CW 90 Participant Notes from the Lectures during the Years 1903-1905
CW 91 Participant Notes from the Lectures during the Years 1903-1905
CW 92 The Occult Truths of Ancient Myths and Sagas
CW 93 The Temple Legend and the Golden Legend
CW 93a Fundamentals of Esotericism
CW 94 Cosmogony. Popular Occultism. The Gospel of John. The Theosophy in the Gospel of John
CW 95 At the Gates of Theosophy
CW 96 Origin-Impulses of Spiritual Science. Christian Esotericism in the Light of New Spirit-Knowledge
CW 97 The Christian Mystery
CW 98 Nature Beings and Spirit Beings—Their Effects in Our Visible World
CW 99 The Theosophy of the Rosicrucians
CW 100 Human Development and Christ-Knowledge
CW 101 Myths and Legends. Occult Signs and Symbols
CW 102 The Working into Human Beings by Spiritual Beings
CW 103 The Gospel of John
CW 104 The Apocalypse of John
CW 104a From the Picture-Script of the Apocalypse of John
CW 105 Universe, Earth, the Human Being: Their Being and Development, as well as Their Reflection in the Connection between Egyptian Mythology and Modern Culture
CW 106 Egyptian Myths and Mysteries in Relation to the Active Spiritual Forces of the Present
CW 107 Spiritual-Scientific Knowledge of the Human Being
CW 108 Answering the Questions of Life and the World through Anthroposophy
CW 109 The Principle of Spiritual Economy in Connection with the Question of Reincarnation. An Aspect of the Spiritual Guidance of Humanity
CW 110 The Spiritual Hierarchies and Their Reflection in the Physical World. Zodiac, Planets and Cosmos

CW 111 Contained in CW 109
CW 112 The Gospel of John in Relation to the Three Other Gospels, Especially the Gospel of Luke
CW 113 The Orient in the Light of the Occident. The Children of Lucifer and the Brothers of Christ
CW 114 The Gospel of Luke
CW 115 Anthroposophy—Psychosophy—Pneumatosophy
CW 116 The Christ-Impulse and the Development of I-Consciousness
CW 117 The Deeper Secrets of the Development of Humanity in Light of the Gospels
CW 118 The Event of the Christ-Appearance in the Etheric World
CW 119 Macrocosm and Microcosm. The Large World and the Small World. Soul-Questions, Life-Questions, Spirit-Questions
CW 120 The Revelation of Karma
CW 121 The Mission of Individual Folk-Souls in Connection with Germanic-Nordic Mythology
CW 122 The Secrets of the Biblical Creation-Story. The Six-Day Work in the First Book of Moses
CW 123 The Gospel of Matthew
CW 124 Excursus in the Area of the Gospel of Mark
CW 125 Paths and Goals of the Spiritual Human Being. Life Questions in the Light of Spiritual Science
CW 126 Occult History. Esoteric Observations of the Karmic Relationships of Personalities and Events of World History
CW 127 The Mission of the New Spiritual Revelation. The Christ-Event as the Middle-Point of Earth Evolution
CW 128 An Occult Physiology
CW 129 Wonders of the World, Trials of the Soul, and Revelations of the Spirit
CW 130 Esoteric Christianity and the Spiritual Guidance of Humanity
CW 131 From Jesus to Christ
CW 132 Evolution from the View Point of the Truth
CW 133 The Earthly and the Cosmic Human Being
CW 134 The World of the Senses and the World of the Spirit
CW 135 Reincarnation and Karma and their Meaning for the Culture of the Present
CW 136 The Spiritual Beings in Celestial Bodies and the Realms of Nature
CW 137 The Human Being in the Light of Occultism, Theosophy and Philosophy
CW 138 On Initiation. On Eternity and the Passing Moment. On the Light of the Spirit and the Darkness of Life
CW 139 The Gospel of Mark
CW 140 Occult Investigation into the Life between Death and New Birth. The Living Interaction between Life and Death
CW 141 Life between Death and New Birth in Relationship to Cosmic Facts

CW 142	The Bhagavad Gita and the Letters of Paul
CW 143	Experiences of the Supersensible. Three Paths of the Soul to Christ
CW 144	The Mysteries of the East and of Christianity
CW 145	What Significance Does Occult Development of the Human Being Have for the Sheaths—Physical Body, Etheric Body, Astral Body, and Self?
CW 146	The Occult Foundations of the Bhagavad Gita
CW 147	The Secrets of the Threshold
CW 148	Out of Research in the Akasha: The Fifth Gospel
CW 149	Christ and the Spiritual World. Concerning the Search for the Holy Grail
CW 150	The World of the Spirit and Its Extension into Physical Existence; The Influence of the Dead in the World of the Living
CW 151	Human Thought and Cosmic Thought
CW 152	Preliminary Stages to the Mystery of Golgotha
CW 153	The Inner Being of the Human Being and Life Between Death and New Birth
CW 154	How Does One Gain an Understanding of the Spiritual World? The Flowing in of Spiritual Impulses from out of the World of the Deceased
CW 155	Christ and the Human Soul. Concerning the Meaning of Life. Theosophical Morality. Anthroposophy and Christianity
CW 156	Occult Reading and Occult Hearing
CW 157	Human Destinies and the Destiny of Peoples
CW 157a	The Formation of Destiny and the Life after Death
CW 158	The Connection Between the Human Being and the Elemental World. Kalevala—Olaf Åsteson—The Russian People—The World as the Result of the Influences of Equilibrium
CW 159	The Mystery of Death. The Nature and Significance of Middle Europe and the European Folk Spirits
CW 160	In CW 159
CW 161	Paths of Spiritual Knowledge and the Renewal of the Artistic Worldview
CW 162	Questions of Art and Life in Light of Spiritual Science
CW 163	Coincidence, Necessity and Providence. Imaginative Knowledge and the Processes after Death
CW 164	The Value of Thinking for a Knowledge That Satisfies the Human Being. The Relationship of Spiritual Science to Natural Science
CW 165	The Spiritual Unification of Humanity through the Christ-Impulse
CW 166	Necessity and Freedom in the Events of the World and in Human Action
CW 167	The Present and the Past in the Human Spirit
CW 168	The Connection between the Living and the Dead
CW 169	World-being and Selfhood
CW 170	The Riddle of the Human Being. The Spiritual Background of Human History. Cosmic and Human History, Vol. 1

CW 171 Inner Development-Impulses of Humanity. Goethe and the Crisis of the 19th Century. Cosmic and Human History, Vol. 2
CW 172 The Karma of the Vocation of the Human Being in Connection with Goethe's Life. Cosmic and Human History, Vol. 3
CW 173 Contemporary-Historical Considerations: The Karma of Untruthfulness, Part One. Cosmic and Human History, Vol. 4
CW 174 Contemporary-Historical Considerations: The Karma of Untruthfulness, Part Two. Cosmic and Human History, Vol. 5
CW 174a Middle Europe between East and West. Cosmic and Human History, Vol. 6
CW 174b The Spiritual Background of the First World War. Cosmic and Human History, Vol. 7
CW 175 Building Stones for an Understanding of the Mystery of Golgotha. Cosmic and Human Metamorphoses
CW 176 Truths of Evolution of the Individual and Humanity. The Karma of Materialism
CW 177 The Spiritual Background of the Outer World. The Fall of the Spirits of Darkness. Spiritual Beings and Their Effects, Vol. 1
CW 178 Individual Spiritual Beings and their Influence in the Soul of the Human Being. Spiritual Beings and their Effects, Vol. 2
CW 179 Spiritual Beings and Their Effects. Historical Necessity and Freedom. The Influences on Destiny from out of the World of the Dead. Spiritual Beings and Their Effects, Vol. 3
CW 180 Mystery Truths and Christmas Impulses. Ancient Myths and their Meaning. Spiritual Beings and Their Effects, Vol. 4
CW 181 Earthly Death and Cosmic Life. Anthroposophical Gifts for Life. Necessities of Consciousness for the Present and the Future.
CW 182 Death as Transformation of Life
CW 183 The Science of the Development of the Human Being
CW 184 The Polarity of Duration and Development in Human Life. The Cosmic Pre-History of Humanity
CW 185 Historical Symptomology
CW 185a Historical-Developmental Foundations for Forming a Social Judgement
CW 186 The Fundamental Social Demands of Our Time—In Changed Situations
CW 187 How Can Humanity Find the Christ Again? The Threefold Shadow-Existence of our Time and the New Christ-Light
CW 188 Goetheanism, a Transformation-Impulse and Resurrection-Thought. Science of the Human Being and Science of Sociology
CW 189 The Social Question as a Question of Consciousness. The Spiritual Background of the Social Question, Vol. 1
CW 190 Impulses of the Past and the Future in Social Occurrences. The Spiritual Background of the Social Question, Vol. 2

CW 191 Social Understanding from Spiritual-Scientific Cognition. The Spiritual Background of the Social Question, Vol. 3
CW 192 Spiritual-Scientific Treatment of Social and Pedagogical Questions
CW 193 The Inner Aspect of the Social Riddle. Luciferic Past and Ahrimanic Future
CW 194 The Mission of Michael. The Revelation of the Actual Mysteries of the Human Being
CW 195 Cosmic New Year and the New Year Idea
CW 196 Spiritual and Social Transformations in the Development of Humanity
CW 197 Polarities in the Development of Humanity: West and East Materialism and Mysticism Knowledge and Belief
CW 198 Healing Factors for the Social Organism
CW 199 Spiritual Science as Knowledge of the Foundational Impulses of Social Formation
CW 200 The New Spirituality and the Christ-Experience of the 20th Century
CW 201 The Correspondences Between Microcosm and Macrocosm. The Human Being—A Hieroglyph of the Universe. The Human Being in Relationship with the Cosmos: 1
CW 202 The Bridge between the World-Spirituality and the Physical Aspect of the Human Being. The Search for the New Isis, the Divine Sophia. The Human Being in Relationship with the Cosmos: 2
CW 203 The Responsibility of Human Beings for the Development of the World through their Spiritual Connection with the Planet Earth and the World of the Stars. The Human Being in Relationship with the Cosmos: 3
CW 204 Perspectives of the Development of Humanity. The Materialistic Knowledge-Impulse and the Task of Anthroposophy. The Human Being in Relationship with the Cosmos: 4
CW 205 Human Development, World-Soul, and World-Spirit. Part One: The Human Being as a Being of Body and Soul in Relationship to the World. The Human Being in Relationship with the Cosmos: 5
CW 206 Human Development, World-Soul, and World-Spirit. Part Two: The Human Being as a Spiritual Being in the Process of Historical Development. The Human Being in Relationship with the Cosmos: 6
CW 207 Anthroposophy as Cosmosophy. Part One: Characteristic Features of the Human Being in the Earthly and the Cosmic Realms. The Human Being in Relationship with the Cosmos: 7
CW 208 Anthroposophy as Cosmosophy. Part Two: The Forming of the Human Being as the Result of Cosmic Influence. The Human Being in Relationship with the Cosmos: 8
CW 209 Nordic and Central European Spiritual Impulses. The Festival of the Appearance of Christ. The Human Being in Relationship with the Cosmos: 9

CW 210 Old and New Methods of Initiation. Drama and Poetry in the Change of Consciousness in the Modern Age
CW 211 The Sun Mystery and the Mystery of Death and Resurrection. Exoteric and Esoteric Christianity
CW 212 Human Soul Life and Spiritual Striving in Connection with World and Earth Development
CW 213 Human Questions and World Answers
CW 214 The Mystery of the Trinity: The Human Being in Relationship with the Spiritual World in the Course of Time
CW 215 Philosophy, Cosmology, and Religion in Anthroposophy
CW 216 The Fundamental Impulses of the World-Historical Development of Humanity
CW 217 Spiritually Active Forces in the Coexistence of the Older and Younger Generations. Pedagogical Course for Youth
CW 217a Youth's Cognitive Task
CW 218 Spiritual Connections in the Forming of the Human Organism
CW 219 The Relationship of the World of the Stars to the Human Being, and of the Human Being to the World of the Stars. The Spiritual Communion of Humanity
CW 220 Living Knowledge of Nature. Intellectual Fall and Spiritual Redemption
CW 221 Earth-Knowing and Heaven-Insight
CW 222 The Imparting of Impulses to World-Historical Events through Spiritual Powers
CW 223 The Cycle of the Year as Breathing Process of the Earth and the Four Great Festival-Seasons. Anthroposophy and the Human Heart (*Gemüt*)
CW 224 The Human Soul and its Connection with Divine-Spiritual Individualities. The Internalization of the Festivals of the Year
CW 225 Three Perspectives of Anthroposophy. Cultural Phenomena observed from a Spiritual-Scientific Perspective
CW 226 Human Being, Human Destiny, and World Development
CW 227 Initiation-Knowledge
CW 228 Science of Initiation and Knowledge of the Stars. The Human Being in the Past, the Present, and the Future from the Viewpoint of the Development of Consciousness
CW 229 The Experiencing of the Course of the Year in Four Cosmic Imaginations
CW 230 The Human Being as Harmony of the Creative, Building, and Formative World-Word
CW 231 The Supersensible Human Being, Understood Anthroposophically
CW 232 The Forming of the Mysteries
CW 233 World History Illuminated by Anthroposophy and as the Foundation for Knowledge of the Human Spirit

CW 233a Mystery Sites of the Middle Ages: Rosicrucianism and the Modern Initiation-Principle. The Festival of Easter as Part of the History of the Mysteries of Humanity
CW 234 Anthroposophy. A Summary after 21 Years
CW 235 Esoteric Observations of Karmic Relationships in 6 Volumes, Vol. 1
CW 236 Esoteric Observations of Karmic Relationships in 6 Volumes, Vol. 2
CW 237 Esoteric Observations of Karmic Relationships in 6 Volumes, Vol. 3: The Karmic Relationships of the Anthroposophical Movement
CW 238 Esoteric Observations of Karmic Relationships in 6 Volumes, Vol. 4: The Spiritual Life of the Present in Relationship to the Anthroposophical Movement
CW 239 Esoteric Observations of Karmic Relationships in 6 Volumes, Vol. 5
CW 240 Esoteric Observations of Karmic Relationships in 6 Volumes, Vol. 6
CW 243 The Consciousness of the Initiate
CW 245 Instructions for an Esoteric Schooling
CW 250 The Building-Up of the Anthroposophical Society. From the Beginning to the Outbreak of the First World War
CW 251 The History of the Goetheanum Building-Association
CW 252 Life in the Anthroposophical Society from the First World War to the Burning of the First Goetheanum
CW 253 The Problems of Living Together in the Anthroposophical Society. On the Dornach Crisis of 1915. With Highlights on Swedenborg's Clairvoyance, the Views of Freudian Psychoanalysts, and the Concept of Love in Relation to Mysticism
CW 254 The Occult Movement in the 19th Century and Its Relationship to World Culture. Significant Points from the Exoteric Cultural Life around the Middle of the 19th Century
CW 255 Rudolf Steiner during the First World War
CW 255a Anthroposophy and the Reformation of Society. On the History of the Threefold Movement
CW 255b Anthroposophy and Its Opponents, 1919–1921
CW 256 How Can the Anthroposophical Movement Be Financed?
CW 256a Futurum, Inc. / International Laboratories, Inc.
CW 256b The Coming Day, Inc.
CW 257 Anthroposophical Community-Building
CW 258 The History of and Conditions for the Anthroposophical Movement in Relationship to the Anthroposophical Society. A Stimulus to Self-Contemplation
CW 259 The Year of Destiny 1923 in the History of the Anthroposophical Society. From the Burning of the Goetheanum to the Christmas Conference
CW 260 The Christmas Conference for the Founding of the General Anthroposophical Society

CW 260a The Constitution of the General Anthroposophical Society and the School for Spiritual Science. The Rebuilding of the Goetheanum
CW 261 Our Dead. Addresses, Words of Remembrance, and Meditative Verses, 1906-1924
CW 262 Rudolf Steiner and Marie Steiner-von Sivers: Correspondence and Documents, 1901-1925
CW 263/1 Rudolf Steiner and Edith Maryon: Correspondence: Letters, Verses, Sketches, 1912-1924
CW 264 On the History and the Contents of the First Section of the Esoteric School from 1904 to 1914. Letters, Newsletters, Documents, Lectures
CW 265 On the History and from the Contents of the Ritual-Knowledge Section of the Esoteric School from 1904 to 1914. Documents, and Lectures from the Years 1906 to 1914, as well as on New Approaches to Ritual-Knowledge Work in the Years 1921–1924
CW 266/1 From the Contents of the Esoteric Lessons. Volume 1: 1904–1909. Notes from Memory of Participants. Meditation texts from the notes of Rudolf Steiner
CW 266/2 From the Contents of the Esoteric Lessons. Volume 2: 1910–1912. Notes from Memory of Participants
CW 266/3 From the Contents of the Esoteric Lessons. Volume 3: 1913, 1914 and 1920–1923. Notes from Memory of Participants. Meditation texts from the notes of Rudolf Steiner
CW 267 Soul-Exercises: Vol. 1: Exercises with Word and Image Meditations for the Methodological Development of Higher Powers of Knowledge, 1904–1924
CW 268 Soul-Exercises: Vol. 2: Mantric Verses, 1903–1925
CW 269 Ritual Texts for the Celebration of the Free Christian Religious Instruction. The Collected Verses for Teachers and Students of the Waldorf School
CW 270 Esoteric Instructions for the First Class of the School for Spiritual Science at the Goetheanum 1924, 4 Volumes
CW 271 Art and Knowledge of Art. Foundations of a New Aesthetic
CW 272 Spiritual-Scientific Commentary on Goethe's 'Faust' in Two Volumes. Vol. 1: Faust, the Striving Human Being
CW 273 Spiritual-Scientific Commentary on Goethe's 'Faust' in Two Volumes. Vol. 2: The Faust-Problem
CW 274 Addresses for the Christmas Plays from the Old Folk Traditions
CW 275 Art in the Light of Mystery-Wisdom
CW 276 The Artistic in Its Mission in the World. The Genius of Language. The World of Self-Revealing Radiant Appearances—Anthroposophy and Art. Anthroposophy and Poetry
CW 277 Eurythmy. The Revelation of the Speaking Soul
CW 277a The Origin and Development of Eurythmy

CW 278	Eurythmy as Visible Song
CW 279	Eurythmy as Visible Speech
CW 280	The Method and Nature of Speech Formation
CW 281	The Art of Recitation and Declamation
CW 282	Speech Formation and Dramatic Art
CW 283	The Nature of Things Musical and the Experience of Tone in the Human Being
CW 284/285	Images of Occult Seals and Pillars. The Munich Congress of Whitsun 1907 and Its Consequences
CW 286	Paths to a New Style of Architecture. 'And the Building Becomes Human'
CW 287	The Building at Dornach as a Symbol of Historical Becoming and an Artistic Transformation Impulse
CW 288	Style-Forms in the Living Organic
CW 289	The Building-Idea of the Goetheanum: Lectures with Slides from the Years 1920–1921
CW 290	The Building-Idea of the Goetheanum: Lectures with Slides from the Years 1920–1921
CW 291	The Nature of Colours
CW 291a	Knowledge of Colours. Supplementary Volume to 'The Nature of Colours'
CW 292	Art History as Image of Inner Spiritual Impulses
CW 293	General Knowledge of the Human Being as the Foundation of Pedagogy
CW 294	The Art of Education, Methodology and Didactics
CW 295	The Art of Education: Seminar Discussions and Lectures on Lesson Planning
CW 296	The Question of Education as a Social Question
CW 297	The Idea and Practice of the Waldorf School
CW 297a	Education for Life: Self-Education and the Practice of Pedagogy
CW 298	Rudolf Steiner in the Waldorf School
CW 299	Spiritual-Scientific Observations on Speech
CW 300a	Conferences with the Teachers of the Free Waldorf School in Stuttgart, 1919 to 1924, in 3 Volumes, Vol. 1
CW 300b	Conferences with the Teachers of the Free Waldorf School in Stuttgart, 1919 to 1924, in 3 Volumes, Vol. 2
CW 300c	Conferences with the Teachers of the Free Waldorf School in Stuttgart, 1919 to 1924, in 3 Volumes, Vol. 3
CW 301	The Renewal of Pedagogical-Didactical Art through Spiritual Science
CW 302	Knowledge of the Human Being and the Forming of Class Lessons
CW 302a	Education and Teaching from a Knowledge of the Human Being
CW 303	The Healthy Development of the Human Being
CW 304	Methods of Education and Teaching Based on Anthroposophy
CW 304a	Anthroposophical Knowledge of the Human Being and Pedagogy

CW 305 The Soul-Spiritual Foundational Forces of the Art of Education. Spiritual Values in Education and Social Life
CW 306 Pedagogical Praxis from the Viewpoint of a Spiritual-Scientific Knowledge of the Human Being. The Education of the Child and Young Human Beings
CW 307 The Spiritual Life of the Present and Education
CW 308 The Method of Teaching and the Life-Requirements for Teaching
CW 309 Anthroposophical Pedagogy and Its Prerequisites
CW 310 The Pedagogical Value of a Knowledge of the Human Being and the Cultural Value of Pedagogy
CW 311 The Art of Education from an Understanding of the Being of Humanity
CW 312 Spiritual Science and Medicine
CW 313 Spiritual-Scientific Viewpoints on Therapy
CW 314 Physiology and Therapy Based on Spiritual Science
CW 315 Curative Eurythmy
CW 316 Meditative Observations and Instructions for a Deepening of the Art of Healing
CW 317 The Curative Education Course
CW 318 The Working Together of Doctors and Pastors
CW 319 Anthroposophical Knowledge of the Human Being and Medicine
CW 320 Spiritual-Scientific Impulses for the Development of Physics 1: The First Natural-Scientific Course: Light, Colour, Tone, Mass, Electricity, Magnetism
CW 321 Spiritual-Scientific Impulses for the Development of Physics 2: The Second Natural-Scientific Course: Warmth at the Border of Positive and Negative Materiality
CW 322 The Borders of the Knowledge of Nature
CW 323 The Relationship of the various Natural-Scientific Fields to Astronomy
CW 324 Nature Observation, Mathematics, and Scientific Experimentation and Results from the Viewpoint of Anthroposophy
CW 324a The Fourth Dimension in Mathematics and Reality
CW 325 Natural Science and the World-Historical Development of Humanity since Ancient Times
CW 326 The Moment of the Coming Into Being of Natural Science in World History and Its Development Since Then
CW 327 Spiritual-Scientific Foundations for Success in Farming. The Agricultural Course
CW 328 The Social Question
CW 329 The Liberation of the Human Being as the Foundation for a New Social Form
CW 330 The Renewal of the Social Organism
CW 331 Work-Council and Socialization
CW 332 The Alliance for Threefolding and the Total Reform of Society. The Council on Culture and the Liberation of the Spiritual Life

CW 332a The Social Future
CW 333 Freedom of Thought and Social Forces
CW 334 From the Unified State to the Threefold Social Organism
CW 335 The Crisis of the Present and the Path to Healthy Thinking
CW 336 The Great Questions of the Times and Anthroposophical Spiritual Knowledge
CW 337a Social Ideas, Social Reality, Social Practice, Vol. 1: Question-and-Answer Evenings and Study Evenings of the Alliance for the Threefold Social Organism in Stuttgart, 1919-1920
CW 337b Social Ideas, Social Realities, Social Practice, Vol. 2: Discussion Evenings of the Swiss Alliance for the Threefold Social Organism
CW 338 How Does One Work on Behalf of the Impulse for the Threefold Social Organism?
CW 339 Anthroposophy, Threefold Social Organism, and the Art of Public Speaking
CW 340 The National-Economics Course. The Tasks of a New Science of Economics, Volume 1
CW 341 The National-Economics Seminar. The Tasks of a New Science of Economics, Volume 2
CW 342 Lectures and Courses on Christian Religious Work, Vol. 1: Anthroposophical Foundations for a Renewed Christian Religious Working
CW 343 Lectures and Courses on Christian Religious Work, Vol. 2: Spiritual Knowledge—Religious Feeling—Cultic Doing
CW 344 Lectures and Courses on Christian Religious Work, Vol. 3: Lectures at the Founding of the Christian Community
CW 345 Lectures and Courses on Christian Religious Work, Vol. 4: Concerning the Nature of the Working Word
CW 346 Lectures and Courses on Christian Religious Work, Vol. 5: The Apocalypse and the Work of the Priest
CW 347 The Knowledge of the Nature of the Human Being According to Body, Soul and Spirit. On Earlier Conditions of the Earth
CW 348 On Health and Illness. Foundations of a Spiritual-Scientific Doctrine of the Senses
CW 349 On the Life of the Human Being and of the Earth. On the Nature of Christianity
CW 350 Rhythms in the Cosmos and in the Human Being. How Does One Come To See the Spiritual World?
CW 351 The Human Being and the World. The Influence of the Spirit in Nature. On the Nature of Bees
CW 352 Nature and the Human Being Observed Spiritual-Scientifically
CW 353 The History of Humanity and the World-Views of the Folk Cultures
CW 354 The Creation of the World and the Human Being. Life on Earth and the Influence of the Stars

SIGNIFICANT EVENTS IN THE LIFE OF RUDOLF STEINER

1829: June 23: birth of Johann Steiner (1829–1910)—Rudolf Steiner's father—in Geras, Lower Austria.

1834: May 8: birth of Franciska Blie (1834–1918)—Rudolf Steiner's mother—in Horn, Lower Austria. 'My father and mother were both children of the glorious Lower Austrian forest district north of the Danube.'

1860: May 16: marriage of Johann Steiner and Franciska Blie.

1861: February 25: birth of *Rudolf Joseph Lorenz Steiner* in Kraljevec, Croatia, near the border with Hungary, where Johann Steiner works as a telegrapher for the South Austria Railroad. Rudolf Steiner is baptized two days later, February 27, the date usually given as his birthday.

1862: Summer: the family moves to Modling, Lower Austria.

1863: The family moves to Pottschach, Lower Austria, near the Styrian border, where Johann Steiner becomes stationmaster. 'The view stretched to the mountains . . . majestic peaks in the distance and the sweet charm of nature in the immediate surroundings.'

1864: November 15: birth of Rudolf Steiner's sister, Leopoldine (d. November 1, 1927). She will become a seamstress and live with her parents for the rest of her life.

1866: July 28: birth of Rudolf Steiner's deaf-mute brother, Gustav (d. May 1, 1941).

1867: Rudolf Steiner enters the village school. Following a disagreement between his father and the schoolmaster, whose wife falsely accused the boy of causing a commotion, Rudolf Steiner is taken out of school and taught at home.

1868: A critical experience. Unknown to the family, an aunt dies in a distant town. Sitting in the station waiting room, Rudolf Steiner sees her 'form', which speaks to him, asking for help. 'Beginning with this experience, a new soul life began in the boy, one in which not only the outer trees and mountains spoke to him, but also the worlds that lay behind them. From this moment on, the boy began to live with the spirits of nature . . .'

1869: The family moves to the peaceful, rural village of Neudorfl, near Wiener Neustadt in present-day Austria. Rudolf Steiner attends the village school. Because of the 'unorthodoxy' of his writing and spelling, he has to do 'extra lessons'.

1870: Through a book lent to him by his tutor, he discovers geometry: 'To grasp something purely in the spirit brought me inner happiness. I know that I first learned happiness through geometry.' The same tutor allows him to draw, while other students still struggle with their reading and writing. 'An artistic element' thus enters his education.

1871: Though his parents are not religious, Rudolf Steiner becomes a 'church child', a favourite of the priest, who was 'an exceptional character'. 'Up to the age of ten or eleven, among those I came to know, he was far and away the most significant.' Among other things, he introduces Steiner to Copernican, heliocentric cosmology. As an altar boy, Rudolf Steiner serves at Masses, funerals, and Corpus Christi processions. At year's end, after an incident in which he escapes a thrashing, his father forbids him to go to church.

1872: Rudolf Steiner transfers to grammar school in Wiener-Neustadt, a five-mile walk from home, which must be done in all weathers.

1873–75: Through his teachers and on his own, Rudolf Steiner has many wonderful experiences with science and mathematics. Outside school, he teaches himself analytic geometry, trigonometry, differential equations, and calculus.

1876: Rudolf Steiner begins tutoring other students. He learns bookbinding from his father. He also teaches himself stenography.

1877: Rudolf Steiner discovers Kant's *Critique of Pure Reason,* which he reads and rereads. He also discovers and reads von Rotteck's *World History.*

1878: He studies extensively in contemporary psychology and philosophy.

1879: Rudolf Steiner graduates from high school with honours. His father is transferred to Inzersdorf, near Vienna. He uses his first visit to Vienna 'to purchase a great number of philosophy books'—Kant, Fichte, Schelling, and Hegel, as well as numerous histories of philosophy. His aim: to find a path from the 'I' to nature.

October
1879–1883: Rudolf Steiner attends the Technical College in Vienna—to study mathematics, chemistry, physics, mineralogy, botany, zoology,

biology, geology, and mechanics—with a scholarship. He also attends lectures in history and literature, while avidly reading philosophy on his own. His two favourite professors are Karl Julius Schröer (German language and literature) and Edmund Reitlinger (physics). He also audits lectures by Robert Zimmermann on aesthetics and Franz Brentano on philosophy. During this year he begins his friendship with Moritz Zitter (1861–1921), who will help support him financially when he is in Berlin.

1880: Rudolf Steiner attends lectures on Schiller and Goethe by Karl Julius Schröer, who becomes his mentor. Also 'through a remarkable combination of circumstances', he meets Felix Koguzki, a 'herb gatherer' and healer, who could 'see deeply into the secrets of nature'. Rudolf Steiner will meet and study with this 'emissary of the Master' throughout his time in Vienna.

1881: January: '... I didn't sleep a wink. I was busy with philosophical problems until about 12:30 a.m. Then, finally, I threw myself down on my couch. All my striving during the previous year had been to research whether the following statement by Schelling was true or not: *Within everyone dwells a secret, marvellous capacity to draw back from the stream of time—out of the self clothed in all that comes to us from outside—into our innermost being and there, in the immutable form of the Eternal, to look into ourselves.* I believe, and I am still quite certain of it, that I discovered this capacity in myself; I had long had an inkling of it. Now the whole of idealist philosophy stood before me in modified form. What's a sleepless night compared to that!'

Rudolf Steiner begins communicating with leading thinkers of the day, who send him books in return, which he reads eagerly.

July: 'I am not one of those who dives into the day like an animal in human form. I pursue a quite specific goal, an idealistic aim—knowledge of the truth! This cannot be done offhandedly. It requires the greatest striving in the world, free of all egotism, and equally of all resignation.'

August: Steiner puts down on paper for the first time thoughts for a 'Philosophy of Freedom'. 'The striving for the absolute: this human yearning is freedom.' He also seeks to outline a 'peasant philosophy', describing what the worldview of a 'peasant'—one who lives close to the earth and the old ways—really is.

1881–1882: Felix Koguzki, the herb gatherer, reveals himself to be the envoy of another, higher initiatory personality, who instructs Rudolf Steiner to penetrate Fichte's philosophy and to master modern scientific thinking as a preparation for right entry into the spirit. This 'Master' also teaches him the double (evolutionary and involutionary) nature of time.

1882: Through the offices of Karl Julius Schröer, Rudolf Steiner is asked by Joseph Kürschner to edit Goethe's scientific works for the *Deutschen National-Literatur* edition. He writes 'A Possible Critique of Atomistic Concepts' and sends it to Friedrich Theodor Vischer.

1883: Rudolf Steiner completes his college studies and begins work on the Goethe project.

1884: First volume of Goethe's *Scientific Writings* (CW 1) appears (March). He lectures on Goethe and Lessing, and Goethe's approach to science. In July, he enters the household of Ladislaus and Pauline Specht as tutor to the four Specht boys. He will live there until 1890. At this time, he meets Josef Breuer (1842–1925), the co-author with Sigmund Freud of *Studies in Hysteria,* who is the Specht family doctor.

1885: While continuing to edit Goethe's writings, Rudolf Steiner reads deeply in contemporary philosophy (Eduard von Hartmann, Johannes Volkelt, and Richard Wahle, among others).

1886: May: Rudolf Steiner sends Kürschner the manuscript of *Outlines of Goethe's Theory of Knowledge* (CW 2), which appears in October, and which he sends out widely. He also meets the poet Marie Eugenie Delle Grazie and writes 'Nature and Our Ideals' for her. He attends her salon, where he meets many priests, theologians, and philosophers, who will become his friends. Meanwhile, the director of the Goethe Archive in Weimar requests his collaboration with the *Sophien* edition of Goethe's works, particularly the writings on colour.

1887: At the beginning of the year, Rudolf Steiner is very sick. As the year progresses and his health improves, he becomes increasingly 'a man of letters', lecturing, writing essays, and taking part in Austrian cultural life. In August–September, the second volume of Goethe's *Scientific Writings* appears.

1888: January–July: Rudolf Steiner assumes editorship of the 'German Weekly' *(Deutsche Wochenschrift)*. He begins lecturing more intensively, giving, for example, a lecture titled 'Goethe as Father of a New Aesthetics'. He meets and becomes soul friends with Friedrich Eckstein (1861–1939), a vegetarian, philosopher of symbolism, alchemist, and musician, who will introduce him to various spiritual currents (including Theosophy) and with whom he will meditate and interpret esoteric and alchemical texts.

1889: Rudolf Steiner first reads Nietzsche *(Beyond Good and Evil)*. He encounters Theosophy again and learns of Madame Blavatsky in the theosophical circle around Marie Lang (1858–1934). Here he also meets well-known figures of Austrian life, as well as esoteric figures like the occultist Franz Hartmann and Karl Leinigen-Billigen (translator of C.G. Harrison's *The Transcendental Universe).* During this period, Steiner first reads A.P. Sinnett's *Esoteric Buddhism* and Mabel Collins's *Light on the Path.* He also begins travelling, visiting Budapest, Weimar, and Berlin (where he meets philosopher Eduard von Hartmann).

1890: Rudolf Steiner finishes Volume 3 of Goethe's scientific writings. He begins his doctoral dissertation, which will become *Truth and Science* (CW 3). He also meets the poet and feminist Rosa Mayreder (1858–1938), with whom he can exchange his most intimate thoughts. In September, Rudolf Steiner moves to Weimar to work in the Goethe-Schiller Archive.

1891: Volume 3 of the Kürschner edition of Goethe appears. Meanwhile, Rudolf Steiner edits Goethe's studies in mineralogy and scientific writings for the *Sophien* edition. He meets Ludwig Laistner of the Cotta Publishing Company, who asks for a book on the basic question of metaphysics. From this will result, ultimately, *The Philosophy of Freedom* (CW 4), which will be published not by Cotta but by Emil Felber. In October, Rudolf Steiner takes the oral exam for a doctorate in philosophy, mathematics, and mechanics at Rostock University, receiving his doctorate on the twenty-sixth. In November, he gives his first lecture on Goethe's 'Fairy Tale' in Vienna.

1892: Rudolf Steiner continues work at the Goethe-Schiller Archive and on his *Philosophy of Freedom. Truth and Science,* his doctoral dissertation, is published. Steiner undertakes to write Introductions to books on Schopenhauer and Jean Paul for Cotta. At year's end, he finds lodging with Anna Eunike, née Schulz (1853 1911), a widow with four daughters and a son. He also develops a friendship with Otto Erich Hartleben (1864–1905) with whom he shares literary interests.

1893: Rudolf Steiner begins his habit of producing many reviews and articles. In March, he gives a lecture titled 'Hypnotism, with Reference to Spiritism'. In September, volume 4 of the Kürschner edition is completed. In November, *The Philosophy of Freedom* appears. This year, too, he meets John Henry Mackay (1864–1933), the anarchist, and Max Stirner, a scholar and biographer.

1894: Rudolf Steiner meets Elisabeth Fürster Nietzsche, the philosopher's sister, and begins to read Nietzsche in earnest, beginning with the as yet unpublished *Antichrist.* He also meets Ernst Haeckel (1834–1919). In the fall, he begins to write *Nietzsche, A Fighter against His Time* (CW 5).

1895: May, *Nietzsche, A Fighter against His Time* appears.

1896: January 22: Rudolf Steiner sees Friedrich Nietzsche for the first and only time. Moves between the Nietzsche and the Goethe-Schiller

Archives, where he completes his work before year's end. He falls out with Elisabeth Förster Nietzsche, thus ending his association with the Nietzsche Archive.

1897: Rudolf Steiner finishes the manuscript of *Goethe's Worldview* (CW 6). He moves to Berlin with Anna Eunike and begins editorship of the *Magazin für Literatur.* From now on, Steiner will write countless reviews, literary and philosophical articles, and so on. He begins lecturing at the 'Free Literary Society'. In September, he attends the Zionist Congress in Basel. He sides with Dreyfus in the Dreyfus affair.

1898: Rudolf Steiner is very active as an editor in the political, artistic, and theatrical life of Berlin. He becomes friendly with John Henry Mackay and poet Ludwig Jacobowski (1868–1900). He joins Jacobowski's circle of writers, artists, and scientists—'The Coming Ones' (*Die Kommenden*)—and contributes lectures to the group until 1903. He also lectures at the 'League for College Pedagogy'. He writes an article for Goethe's sesquicentennial, 'Goethe's Secret Revelation', on the 'Fairy Tale of the Green Snake and the Beautiful Lily'.

1898–99: 'This was a trying time for my soul as I looked at Christianity. . . . I was able to progress only by contemplating, by means of spiritual perception, the evolution of Christianity. . . . Conscious knowledge of real Christianity began to dawn in me around the turn of the century. This seed continued to develop. My soul trial occurred shortly before the beginning of the twentieth century. It was decisive for my soul's development that I stood spiritually before the Mystery of Golgotha in a deep and solemn celebration of knowledge.'

1899: Rudolf Steiner begins teaching and giving lectures and lecture cycles at the Workers' College, founded by Wilhelm Liebknecht (1826–1900). He will continue to do so until 1904. Writes: *Literature and Spiritual Life in the Nineteenth Century; Individualism in Philosophy; Haeckel and His Opponents; Poetry in the Present;* and begins what will become (fifteen years later) *The Riddles of Philosophy* (CW 18). He also meets many artists and writers, including Käthe Kollwitz, Stefan Zweig, and Rainer Maria Rilke. On October 31, he marries Anna Eunike.

1900: 'I thought that the turn of the century must bring humanity a new light. It seemed to me that the separation of human thinking and willing from the spirit had peaked. A turn or reversal of direction in human evolution seemed to me a necessity.' Rudolf Steiner finishes *World and Life Views in the Nineteenth Century* (the second part of what will become *The Riddles of Philosophy*) and dedicates it to

Ernst Haeckel. It is published in March. He continues lecturing at *Die Kommenden,* whose leadership he assumes after the death of Jacobowski. Also, he gives the Gutenberg Jubilee lecture before 7,000 typesetters and printers. In September, Rudolf Steiner is invited by Count and Countess Brockdorff to lecture in the Theosophical Library. His first lecture is on Nietzsche. His second lecture is titled 'Goethe's Secret Revelation'. October 6, he begins a lecture cycle on the mystics that will become *Mystics after Modernism* (CW 7). November–December: 'Marie von Sivers appears in the audience. . . .' Also in November, Steiner gives his first lecture at the Giordano Bruno Bund (where he will continue to lecture until May, 1905). He speaks on Bruno and modern Rome, focusing on the importance of the philosophy of Thomas Aquinas as monism.

1901: In continual financial straits, Rudolf Steiner's early friends Moritz Zitter and Rosa Mayreder help support him. In October, he begins the lecture cycle *Christianity as Mystical Fact* (CW 8) at the Theosophical Library. In November, he gives his first 'theosophical lecture' on Goethe's 'Fairy Tale' in Hamburg at the invitation of Wilhelm Hubbe-Schleiden. He also attends a gathering to celebrate the founding of the Theosophical Society at Count and Countess Brockdorff's. He gives a lecture cycle, 'From Buddha to Christ', for the circle of the *Kommenden.* November 17, Marie von Sivers asks Rudolf Steiner if Theosophy needs a Western–Christian spiritual movement (to complement Theosophy's Eastern emphasis). 'The question was posed. Now, following spiritual laws, I could begin to give an answer. . . .' In December, Rudolf Steiner writes his first article for a theosophical publication. At year's end, the Brockdorffs and possibly Wilhelm Hubbe-Schleiden ask Rudolf Steiner to join the Theosophical Society and undertake the leadership of the German Section. Rudolf Steiner agrees, on the condition that Marie von Sivers (then in Italy) work with him.

1902: Beginning in January, Rudolf Steiner attends the opening of the Workers' School in Spandau with Rosa Luxemberg (1870–1919). January 17, Rudolf Steiner joins the Theosophical Society. In April, he is asked to become general secretary of the German Section of the Theosophical Society, and works on preparations for its founding. In July, he visits London for a theosophical congress. He meets Bertram Keightly, G.R.S. Mead, A.P. Sinnett, and Annie Besant, among others. In September, *Christianity as Mystical Fact* appears. In October, Rudolf Steiner gives his first public lecture on Theosophy ('Monism and Theosophy') to about three hundred people at the Giordano Bruno Bund. On October 19–21, the

German Section of the Theosophical Society has its first meeting; Rudolf Steiner is the general secretary, and Annie Besant attends. Steiner lectures on practical karma studies. On October 23, Annie Besant inducts Rudolf Steiner into the Esoteric School of the Theosophical Society. On October 25, Steiner begins a weekly series of lectures: 'The Field of Theosophy'. During this year, Rudolf Steiner also first meets Ita Wegman (1876–1943), who will become his close collaborator in his final years.

1903: Rudolf Steiner holds about 300 lectures and seminars. In May, the first issue of the periodical *Luzifer* appears. In June, Rudolf Steiner visits London for the first meeting of the Federation of the European Sections of the Theosophical Society, where he meets Colonel Olcott. He begins to write *Theosophy* (CW 9).

1904: Rudolf Steiner continues lecturing at the Workers' College and elsewhere (about 90 lectures), while lecturing intensively all over Germany among theosophists (about 140 lectures). In February, he meets Carl Unger (1878–1929), who will become a member of the board of the Anthroposophical Society (1913). In March, he meets Michael Bauer (1871–1929), a Christian mystic, who will also be on the board. In May, *Theosophy* appears, with the dedication: 'To the spirit of Giordano Bruno'. Rudolf Steiner and Marie von Sivers visit London for meetings with Annie Besant. June: Rudolf Steiner and Marie von Sivers attend the meeting of the Federation of European Sections of the Theosophical Society in Amsterdam. In July, Steiner begins the articles in *Luzifer-Gnosis* that will become *How to Know Higher Worlds* (CW 10) and *Cosmic Memory* (CW 11). In September, Annie Besant visits Germany. In December, Steiner lectures on Freemasonry. He mentions the High Grade Masonry derived from John Yarker and represented by Theodore Reuss and Karl Kellner as a blank slate 'into which a good image could be placed'.

1905: This year, Steiner ends his non-theosophical lecturing activity. Supported by Marie von Sivers, his theosophical lecturing—both in public and in the Theosophical Society—increases significantly: 'The German Theosophical Movement is of exceptional importance.' Steiner recommends reading, among others, Fichte, Jacob Boehme, and Angelus Silesius. He begins to introduce Christian themes into Theosophy. He also begins to work with doctors (Felix Peipers and Ludwig Noll). In July, he is in London for the Federation of European Sections, where he attends a lecture by Annie Besant: 'I have seldom seen Mrs Besant speak in so inward and heartfelt a manner... Through Mrs Besant I have found the way to H.P. Blavatsky.' September to October, he gives a course of 31 lectures for a small group of esoteric students. In October, the annual meeting of the German Section of the Theosophical Society, which still remains very small, takes place. Rudolf Steiner reports membership has risen from 121 to 377 members. In November, seeking to establish esoteric 'continuity', Rudolf Steiner and Marie von Sivers participate in a 'Memphis-Misraim' Masonic ceremony. They pay 45 marks for membership. 'Yesterday, you saw how little remains of former esoteric institutions.' 'We are dealing only with a "framework" . . . for the present, nothing lies behind it. The occult powers have completely withdrawn.'

1906: Expansion of theosophical work. Rudolf Steiner gives about 245 lectures, only 44 of which take place in Berlin. Cycles are given in Paris, Leipzig, Stuttgart, and Munich. Esoteric work also intensifies. Rudolf Steiner begins writing *An Outline of Esoteric Science* (CW 13). In January, Rudolf Steiner receives permission (a patent) from the Great Orient of the Scottish A & A Thirty-Three Degree Rite of the Order of the Ancient Freemasons of the Memphis-Misraim Rite to direct a chapter under the name 'Mystica Aeterna'. This will become the 'Cognitive-Ritual Section' (also called 'Misraim Service') of the Esoteric School. (See: *Freemasonry and Ritual Work: The Misraim Service,* CW 265.) During this time, Steiner also meets Albert Schweitzer. In May, he is in Paris, where he visits Édouard Schuré. Many Russians attend his lectures (including Konstantin Balmont, Dimitri Mereszkovski, Zinaida Hippius, and Maximilian Woloshin). He attends the General Meeting of the European Fed eration of the Theosophical Society, at which Col Olcott is present for the last time. He spends the year's end in Venice and Rome, where he writes and works on his translation of H.P. Blavatsky's *Key to Theosophy.*

1907: Further expansion of the German Theosophical Movement according to the Rosicrucian directive to 'introduce spirit into the world'—in education, in social questions, in art, and in science. In February, Col Olcott dies in Adyar. Before he dies, Olcott indicates that 'the Masters' wish Annie Besant to succeed him: much politicking ensues. Rudolf Steiner supports Besant's candidacy. April–May: preparations for the Congress of the Federation of European Sections of the Theosophical Society—the great, watershed Whitsun 'Munich Congress,' attended by Annie Besant and others. Steiner decides to separate Eastern and Western (Christian–Rosicrucian) esoteric schools. He takes his esoteric school out of the Theosophical Society (Besant and Rudolf Steiner are 'in harmony' on this). Steiner makes his first lecture tours to Austria and

Hungary. That summer, he is in Italy. In September, he visits Édouard Schuré, who will write the Introduction to the French edition of *Christianity as Mystical Fact* in Barr, Alsace. Rudolf Steiner writes the autobiographical statement known as the 'Barr Document'. In *Luzifer-Gnosis*, 'The Education of the Child' appears.

1908: The movement grows (membership: 1,150). Lecturing expands. Steiner makes his first extended lecture tour to Holland and Scandinavia, as well as visits to Naples and Sicily. Themes: St John's Gospel, the Apocalypse, Egypt, science, philosophy, and logic. *Luzifer-Gnosis* ceases publication. In Berlin, Marie von Sivers (with Johanna Mücke (1864–1949) forms the *Philosophisch-Theosophisch* (after 1915 *Philosophisch-Anthroposophisch) Verlag* to publish Steiner's work. Steiner gives lecture cycles titled *The Gospel of St John* (CW 103) and *The Apocalypse* (104).

1909: *An Outline of Esoteric Science* appears. Lecturing and travel continues. Rudolf Steiner's spiritual research expands to include the polarity of Lucifer and Ahriman; the work of great individualities in history; the Maitreya Buddha and the Bodhisattvas; spiritual economy (CW 109); the work of the spiritual hierarchies in heaven and on earth (CW 110). He also deepens and intensifies his research into the Gospels, giving lectures on the Gospel of St Luke (CW 114) with the first mention of two Jesus children. Meets and becomes friends with Christian Morgenstern (1871–1914). In April, he lays the foundation stone for the Malsch model—the building that will lead to the first Goetheanum. In May, the International Congress of the Federation of European Sections of the Theosophical Society takes place in Budapest. Rudolf Steiner receives the Subba Row medal for *How to Know Higher Worlds*. During this time, Charles W. Leadbeater discovers Jiddu Krishnamurti (1895–1986) and proclaims him the future 'world teacher', the bearer of the Maitreya Buddha and the 'reappearing Christ'. In October, Steiner delivers seminal lectures on 'anthroposophy', which he will try, unsuccessfully, to rework over the next years into the unfinished work, *Anthroposophy (A Fragment)* (CW 45).

1910: New themes: *The Reappearance of Christ in the Etheric* (CW 118); *The Fifth Gospel; The Mission of Folk Souls* (CW 121); *Occult History* (CW 126); the evolving development of etheric cognitive capacities. Rudolf Steiner continues his Gospel research with *The Gospel of St Matthew* (CW 123). In January, his father dies. In April, he takes a month-long trip to Italy, including Rome, Monte Cassino, and Sicily. He also visits Scandinavia again. July–August, he writes the first Mystery Drama, *The Portal of Initiation* (CW 14). In November, he gives 'psychosophy' lectures. In December, he submits 'On the

Psychological Foundations and Epistemological Framework of Theosophy' to the International Philosophical Congress in Bologna.

1911: The crisis in the Theosophical Society deepens. In January, 'The Order of the Rising Sun', which will soon become 'The Order of the Star in the East', is founded for the coming world teacher, Krishnamurti. At the same time, Marie von Sivers, Rudolf Steiner's co-worker, falls ill. Fewer lectures are given, but important new ground is broken. In Prague, in March, Steiner meets Franz Kafka (1883–1924) and Hugo Bergmann (1883–1975). In April, he delivers his paper to the Philosophical Congress. He writes the second Mystery Drama, *The Soul's Probation* (CW 14). Also, while Marie von Sivers is convalescing, Rudolf Steiner begins work on *Calendar 1912/1913*, which will contain the 'Calendar of the Soul' meditations. On March 19, Anna (Eunike) Steiner dies. In September, Rudolf Steiner visits Einsiedeln, birthplace of Paracelsus. In December, Friedrich Rittelmeyer, future founder of The Christian Community, meets Rudolf Steiner. The *Johannes-Bauverein,* the 'building committee', which would lead to the first Goetheanum (first planned for Munich), is also founded, and a preliminary committee for the founding of an independent association is created that, in the following year, will become the Anthroposophical Society. Important lecture cycles include *Occult Physiology* (CW 128); *Wonders of the World* (CW 129); *From Jesus to Christ* (CW 131). Other themes: esoteric Christianity; Christian Rosenkreutz; the spiritual guidance of humanity; the sense world and the world of the spirit.

1912: Despite the ongoing, now increasing crisis in the Theosophical Society, much is accomplished: *Calendar 1912/1913* is published; eurythmy is created; both the third Mystery Drama, *The Guardian of the Threshold* (CW 14) and *A Way of Self-Knowledge* (CW 16) are written. New (or renewed) themes included life between death and rebirth and karma and reincarnation. Other lecture cycles: *Spiritual Beings in the Heavenly Bodies and in the Kingdoms of Nature* (CW 136); *The Human Being in the Light of Occultism, Theosophy, and Philosophy* (CW 137); *The Gospel of St Mark* (CW 139); and *The Bhagavad Gita and the Epistles of Paul* (CW 142). On May 8, Rudolf Steiner celebrates White Lotus Day, H.P. Blavatsky's death day, which he had faithfully observed for the past decade, for the last time. In August, Rudolf Steiner suggests the 'independent association' be called the 'Anthroposophical Society'. In September, the first eurythmy course takes place. In October, Rudolf Steiner declines recognition of a Theosophical Society Lodge dedicated to the Star of the East and decides to expel all Theosophical Society members belonging to the Order.

Also, with Marie von Sivers, he first visits Dornach, near Basel, Switzerland, and they stand on the hill where the Goetheanum will be built. In November, a Theosophical Society Lodge is opened by direct mandate from Adyar (Annie Besant). In December, a meeting of the German section occurs at which it is decided that belonging to the Order of the Star of the East is incompatible with membership in the Theosophical Society. December 28: informal founding of the Anthroposophical Society in Berlin.

1913: Expulsion of the German section from the Theosophical Society. February 2–3: Foundation meeting of the Anthroposophical Society. Board members include: Marie von Sivers, Michael Bauer, and Carl Unger. September 20: Laying of the foundation stone for the *Johannes Bau* (Goetheanum) in Dornach. Building begins immediately. The fourth Mystery Drama, *The Soul's Awakening* (CW 14), is completed. Also: *The Threshold of the Spiritual World* (CW 147). Lecture cycles include: *The Bhagavad Gita and the Epistles of Paul* and *The Esoteric Meaning of the Bhagavad Gita* (CW 146), which the Russian philosopher Nikolai Berdyaev attends; *The Mysteries of the East and of Christianity* (CW 144); *The Effects of Esoteric Development* (CW 145); and *The Fifth Gospel* (CW 148). In May, Rudolf Steiner is in London and Paris, where anthroposophical work continues.

1914: Building continues on the *Johannes Bau* (Goetheanum) in Dornach, with artists and co-workers from seventeen nations. The General Assembly of the Anthroposophical Society takes place. In May, Rudolf Steiner visits Paris, as well as Chartres Cathedral. June 28: assassination in Sarajevo ('Now the catastrophe has happened!'). August 1: War is declared. Rudolf Steiner returns to Germany from Dornach—he will travel back and forth. He writes the last chapter of *The Riddles of Philosophy*. Lecture cycles include: *Human and Cosmic Thought* (CW 151); *Inner Being of Humanity between Death and a New Birth* (CW 153); *Occult Reading and Occult Hearing* (CW 156). December 24: marriage of Rudolf Steiner and Marie von Sivers.

1915: Building continues. Life after death becomes a major theme, also art. Writes: *Thoughts during a Time of War* (CW 24). Lectures include: *The Secret of Death* (CW 159); *The Uniting of Humanity through the Christ Impulse* (CW 165).

1916: Rudolf Steiner begins work with Edith Maryon (1872–1924) on the sculpture 'The Representative of Humanity' ('The Group'—Christ, Lucifer, and Ahriman). He also works with the alchemist Alexander von Bernus on the quarterly *Das Reich*. He writes *The Riddle of Humanity* (CW 20). Lectures include: *Necessity and Freedom in World History and Human Action* (CW 166); *Past and Present in the*

Human Spirit (CW 167); *The Karma of Vocation* (CW 172); *The Karma of Untruthfulness* (CW 173).

1917: Russian Revolution. The U.S. enters the war. Building continues. Rudolf Steiner delineates the idea of the 'threefold nature of the human being' (in a public lecture March 15) and the 'threefold nature of the social organism' (hammered out in May–June with the help of Otto von Lerchenfeld and Ludwig Polzer-Hoditz in the form of two documents titled *Memoranda,* which were distributed in high places). August–September: Rudolf Steiner writes *The Riddles of the Soul* (CW 20). Also: commentary on 'The Chymical Wedding of Christian Rosenkreutz' for Alexander Bernus (Das *Reich*). Lectures include: *The Karma of Materialism* (CW 176); *The Spiritual Background of the Outer World: The Fall of the Spirits of Darkness* (CW 177).

1918: March 18: peace treaty of Brest-Litovsk—'Now everything will truly enter chaos! What is needed is cultural renewal.' June: Rudolf Steiner visits Karlstein (Grail) Castle outside Prague. Lecture cycle: *From Symptom to Reality in Modern History* (CW 185). In mid-November, Emil Molt, of the Waldorf-Astoria Cigarette Company, has the idea of founding a school for his workers' children.

1919: Focus on the threefold social organism: tireless travel, countless lectures, meetings, and publications. At the same time, a new public stage of Anthroposophy emerges as cultural renewal begins. The coming years will see initiatives in pedagogy, medicine, pharmacology, and agriculture. January 27: threefold meeting: 'We must first of all, with the money we have, found free schools that can bring people what they need.' February: first public eurythmy performance in Zurich. Also: 'Appeal to the German People' (CW 24), circulated March 6 as a newspaper insert. In April, *Towards Social Renewal* (CW 23) appears—'perhaps the most widely read of all books on politics appearing since the war'. Rudolf Steiner is asked to undertake the 'direction and leadership' of the school founded by the Waldorf-Astoria Company. Rudolf Steiner begins to talk about the 'renewal' of education. May 30: a building is selected and purchased for the future Waldorf School. August–September, Rudolf Steiner gives a lecture course for Waldorf teachers, *The Foundations of Human Experience (Study of Man)* (CW 293). September 7: Opening of the first Waldorf School. December (into January): first science course, the *Light Course* (CW 320).

1920: The Waldorf School flourishes. New threefold initiatives. Founding of limited companies *Der Kommende Tag* and *Futurum A.G.* to infuse spiritual values into the economic realm. Rudolf Steiner also focuses on the sciences. Lectures: *Introducing Anthroposophical*

Medicine (CW 312); *The Warmth Course* (CW 321); *The Boundaries of Natural Science* (CW 322); *The Redemption of Thinking* (CW 74). February: Johannes Werner Klein—later a co-founder of The Christian Community—asks Rudolf Steiner about the possibility of a 'religious renewal', a 'Johannine church'. In March, Rudolf Steiner gives the first course for doctors and medical students. In April, a divinity student asks Rudolf Steiner a second time about the possibility of religious renewal. September 27–October 16: anthroposophical 'university course'. December: lectures titled *The Search for the New Isis* (CW 202).

1921: Rudolf Steiner continues his intensive work on cultural renewal, including the uphill battle for the threefold social order. 'University' arts, scientific, theological, and medical courses include: *The Astronomy Course* (CW 323); *Observation, Mathematics, and Scientific Experiment* (CW 324); the *Second Medical Course* (CW 313); *Colour*. In June and September–October, Rudolf Steiner also gives the first two 'priests' courses' (CW 342 and 343). The 'youth movement' gains momentum. Magazines are founded: *Die Drei* (January), and—under the editorship of Albert Steffen (1884–1963)—the weekly, *Das Goetheanum* (August). In February–March, Rudolf Steiner takes his first trip outside Germany since the war (Holland). On April 7, Steiner receives a letter regarding 'religious renewal', and May 22–23, he agrees to address the question in a practical way. In June, the Klinical-Therapeutic Institute opens in Arlesheim under the direction of Dr Ita Wegman. In August, the Chemical-Pharmaceutical Laboratory opens in Arlesheim (Oskar Schmiedel and Ita Wegman are directors). The Clinical Therapeutic Institute is inaugurated in Stuttgart (Dr Ludwig Noll is director); also the Research Laboratory in Dornach (Ehrenfried Pfeiffer and Gunther Wachsmuth are directors). In November–December, Rudolf Steiner visits Norway.

1922: The first half of the year involves very active public lecturing (thousands attend); in the second half, Rudolf Steiner begins to withdraw and turn toward the Society—'The Society is asleep.' It is 'too weak' to do what is asked of it. The businesses—*Der Kommende Tag* and *Futurum A.G.*—fail. In January, with the help of an agent, Steiner undertakes a twelve-city German lecture tour, accompanied by eurythmy performances. In two weeks he speaks to more than 2,000 people. In April, he gives a 'university course' in The Hague. He also visits England. In June, he is in Vienna for the East–West Congress. In August–September, he is back in England for the Oxford Conference on Education. Returning to Dornach, he gives the lectures *Philosophy, Cosmology, and Religion*

(CW 215), and gives the third priests' course (CW 344). On September 16, The Christian Community is founded. In October–November, Steiner is in Holland and England. He also speaks to the youth: *The Youth Course* (CW 217). In December, Steiner gives lectures titled *The Origins of Natural Science* (CW 326), and *Humanity and the World of Stars: The Spiritual Communion of Humanity* (CW 219). December 31: Fire at the Goetheanum, which is destroyed.

1923: Despite the fire, Rudolf Steiner continues his work unabated. A very hard year. Internal dispersion, dissension, and apathy abound. There is conflict—between old and new visions—within the Society. A wake-up call is needed, and Rudolf Steiner responds with renewed lecturing vitality. His focus: the spiritual context of human life; initiation science; the course of the year; and community building. As a foundation for an artistic school, he creates a series of pastel sketches. Lecture cycles: *The Anthroposophical Movement; Initiation Science* (CW 227) (in Wales at the Penmaenmawr Summer School); *The Four Seasons and the Archangels* (CW 229); *Harmony of the Creative Word* (CW 230); *The Supersensible Human* (CW 231), given in Holland for the founding of the Dutch Society. On November 10, in response to the failed Hitler-Ludendorff putsch in Munich, Steiner closes his Berlin residence and moves the *Philosophisch-Anthroposophisch Verlag* (Press) to Dornach. On December 9, Steiner begins the serialization of his *Autobiography: The Course of My Life* (CW 28) in *Das Goetheanum*. It will continue to appear weekly, without a break, until his death. Late December–early January: Rudolf Steiner re-founds the Anthroposophical Society (about 12,000 members internationally) and takes over its leadership. The new board members are: Marie Steiner, Ita Wegman, Albert Steffen, Elisabeth Vreede, and Gunther Wachsmuth. (See *The Christmas Meeting for the Founding of the General Anthroposophical Society*, CW 260.) Accompanying lectures: *Mystery Knowledge and Mystery Centres* (CW 232); *World History in the Light of Anthroposophy* (CW 233). December 25: the Foundation Stone is laid (in the hearts of members) in the form of the 'Foundation Stone Meditation'.

1924: January 1: having founded the Anthroposophical Society and taken over its leadership, Rudolf Steiner has the task of 'reforming' it. The process begins with a weekly newssheet ('What's Happening in the Anthroposophical Society') in which Rudolf Steiner's 'Letters to Members' and 'Anthroposophical Leading Thoughts' appear (CW 26). The next step is the creation of a new esoteric class, the 'first class' of the 'University of Spiritual Science' (which was to have been followed, had Rudolf Steiner lived longer, by two more advanced classes). Then comes a new language for

Anthroposophy—practical, phenomenological, and direct; and Rudolf Steiner creates the model for the second Goetheanum. He begins the series of extensive 'karma' lectures (CW 235–40); and finally, responding to needs, he creates two new initiatives: biodynamic agriculture and curative education. After the middle of the year, rumours begin to circulate regarding Steiner's health. Lectures: January–February, *Anthroposophy* (CW 234); February: *Tone Eurythmy* (CW 278); June: *The Agriculture Course* (CW 327); June–July: *Speech Eurythmy* (CW 279); *Curative Education* (CW 317); August: (England, 'Second International Summer School'), *Initiation Consciousness: True and False Paths in Spiritual Investigation* (CW 243); September: *Pastoral Medicine* (CW 318). On September 26, for the first time, Rudolf Steiner cancels a lecture. On September 28, he gives his last lecture. On September 29, he withdraws to his studio in the carpenter's shop; now he is definitively ill. Cared for by Ita Wegman, he continues working, however, and writing the weekly installments of his *Autobiography* and *Letters to the Members/ Leading Thoughts* (CW 26).

1925: Rudolf Steiner, while continuing to work, continues to weaken. He finishes *Extending Practical Medicine* (CW 27) with Ita Wegman. On March 30, around ten in the morning, Rudolf Steiner dies.

Index

D

E

T

V

W

Y

Z